The BURMA Letters

Lives in the Letters of Tom and Vera Ashley

Janet Powell

Published by

Running Fox
Barton St David

First published 2005

ISBN 0-9550626-0-8

Printed by
The Somerton Printery Ltd,
Somerton, Somerset TA11 7NT

Contents

Dedication

This book is for our children and grandchildren.
It is dedicated to the memory of
Tom, Vera and Roger Ashley.

Acknowledgements

When I started this book I knew nothing about the Burma Campaign and I can now claim only to know a little. I relied upon information from the publications listed in the bibliography and I have quoted particularly from books written by participants in, and observers of, the Campaign. The map of Burma is courtesy of Julian Thompson and I am grateful for his permission to use this. Other sources reveal different perspectives on the effects of war upon people and populations. Any errors of interpretation are entirely my own.

I very much appreciate the advice I have received from staff at the Burma Star Association, the Army Records Office and the Imperial War Museum. I also appreciate the professional help I have been given, so pleasantly, by staff at The Somerton Printery in relation to making the book.

I am grateful for information and photographs supplied by members of the family. Also to Teddy Motler and to Diana Findlay, because their work encouraged me to begin to put this book together, and to my immediate family who gave me the confidence to complete it. Good friends have also helped so much with general support, proof-reading and technical advice. To those who may be reading this now, your comments and encouragement have been invaluable and I thank you.

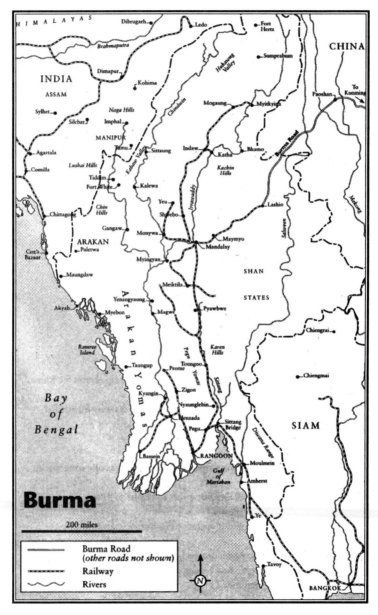

Map of Burma, 1945

Preface

In August 1945 the Second World War finally came to an end with the surrender of Japan, although for many people the war had ended with victory in Europe three months earlier. My father had been away from his home and family for over three years and it was still to be a further four months before he returned.

Since my mother's death, I have gradually read through the letters that they exchanged. Earlier letters reveal how they met during the first year of the war. Later ones were written while Tom was in India and then in Burma. Many people probably have such letters in their family, although it may be less common for collections numbering more than five hundred to survive intact. Together with photographs, they provide a detailed picture of the parallel lives led by Tom and Vera during his absence and they reveal their hopes and concerns about the process of bringing those lives together again.

I always knew where the letters were kept and once tried to read them while I was living at home. My mother stopped me, saying, 'You can read them one day'. Vera could have destroyed the letters or asked that they be kept private. However, she did not do so. In 1942 they decided that they would keep the letters instead of diaries. On the 18th March 1945 she wrote to Tom, 'What shall we do with all our letters after the war darling? Shall we have them bound in a huge volume as a memento of the years we spent apart?' She was proud of their story and of the survival of love and hope throughout almost four years of separation.

To put the letters into context, I have sketched in some background information about the war – a theatre of war so complex, and fought over so many arenas, that it is difficult to describe succinctly. The images and scenes I have selected are those which most directly involved Tom and Vera, events about which they wrote to each other and in the light of which they talked about what the future might hold for them.

The true scale of the Burma campaign, and the terrain of Burma itself, can be fully appreciated only by examining contemporary accounts, maps and descriptions. Owen says, 'Burma interposes itself between the rest of Malaya and India; also between Southern China and India. It is not a corridor but a barrier. This is the military significance of Burma and that is why there was a Burma campaign.' The Battle of Kohima is described by Sir William Slim as having been 'probably one of the greatest battles in history.'

This book, a collection of edited sections of The Burma Letters, other family letters and reminiscences, source material and photographs is a tribute to my parents and to others of their generation who gave so much; sometimes everything.

Janet Powell   **Barton St David 2005**

The Families – 1880 – 1945

The Ashley Family at Oakfield Farm

1. Frederick Ashley [b.1882 d. 1958] *m.1908* Ada Rebekah Johnson [b.1884 d.1979]

2. Mary Bessie [b.1909 d.1985]

2. Frederick [Eric] [b.1911 d.1970]

2. Geoffrey Thomas [Tom] [b.1913 d.1972]

2. Harold Joseph [b.1918 d.1959]

2. Barbara Johnson [b.1928] niece and foster daughter of Fred and Ada

2. Bessie married Laurence [Laurie] Motler 1935

3. Sheila [b.1937], Edward Laurence [Teddy] [b.1939], David [b.1940]

2. Eric married Dorothy [Dot] Simister 1935

3. Tony [b.1936], Bill [b.1938]

2. Tom married Vera Ashton 1940

3. Janet [b.1941]

2. Harold married Marjorie 1945

The Ashton Family in Buxton

1. Roger Evans Ashton [b.1880 d.1949] *m.1907* Emma Slack [b.1880 d. 1967]

2. Frederick [Freddy] - [b.1908 – d.1914]

2. Vera [b.1917 – d.1992]

2. Joyce [b.1921]

2. Vera and Tom married August 1940

2. Joyce married George Blackburn in 1946

Cousins born after 1945

3. **Diana** Cathryn [b.1947] - daughter of Eric and Dot.

3. **Helen** Christine [b.1946], **Roger** Geoffrey John [b.1948 – d.1995] and Jonathan George [**Jonnie or Jon**] [b.1952] – children of Tom and Vera

3. **Peter** [b.1946] – son of Joyce and George Blackburn

3. **David** John [b.1948], **Judith** [b.1949] and Elizabeth [**Liz**] [b. 1956] – children of Harold and Marjorie

Tom and Vera's children, grandchildren and great-grandchildren

*3. Janet married **Dennis** Powell in July 1964*

4. Alwyn **Simon** [b.1967], **Karen** Jane [b.1969] and **Juliet** Clare [b.1973]

*4. Simon m. **Juliet** Emsley in April 1994*

5. **Jack** [b.1993], **Poppy** [b.1996], **Isobel** [b.1999] and **George and Alice** [twins b. 2003]

*4. Karen m. **John** Dixon in July 1994*

5. **Molly** [b.1996] and **Lucy** [b. 2000]

*4. Juliet, partner of **Craig** Lamberton 1998 - 2002*

5. **Callum** [b.2000]

*3. Helen married **Mike** Thomas in August 1975*

4. **Sarah** [b.1978], **Katy** [b.1982] and **Matthew [b.1987]**

*3. Jonathan married **Carol** Cooper in July 1971*

Young Doctor

CHAPTER ONE
January to July 1940

The likelihood of war with Germany had been looming since 1935. Conscription was introduced there and Germany began to arm herself in defiance of the Treaty of Versailles, while the image of the swastika was adopted as the official flag of the country. Following the Nuremburg Rally, stringent laws were announced forbidding marriage between Jews and Aryans. Further threatening moves took place in 1936, particularly the occupation of the Rhineland.

There was high unemployment and much hardship in Britain. 1936 became known as the year of the three kings; George V died; Edward VIII acceded to the throne in January and abdicated, in favour of his brother George VI, in December. There was unrest across the world. In July 1936, the Spanish Civil War erupted and continued until March 1939. In 1937, fierce conflict was taking place between China and Japan. In November 1937, there was sufficient concern about approaching conflict to promote the introduction of an Air Raid Precautions Bill in the House of Commons.

Throughout 1938, Hitler pushed the boundaries by infiltrating further and further into Eastern Europe. Prime Minister Chamberlain negotiated with Hitler at the Munich Conference in September. He returned to England saying that he had achieved 'peace with honour, peace in our time.' Several foremost politicians, notably Winston Churchill, vociferously expressed their disagreement with Chamberlain. In Germany, by the end of the year, Jewish homes, places of worship and property were being systematically burned and looted with impunity.

Threatening moves continued and escalated through 1939. Conscription was introduced in Britain and men aged 18 to 41 were called up into the Services. In August, an Emergency Powers Bill was passed in Parliament. The Germans entered into a pact with the Russians and invaded Poland from the West on September 1st.

On September 3rd, Britain and France declared war on Germany. On the 17th, the Soviet Union invaded Poland from the East. A war cabinet was formed, with Churchill as First Lord of the Admiralty.

Air raid warning sirens were heard for the first time, although no attack immediately ensued. The evacuation of women and children to the country began.

Tom, a newly qualified doctor and houseman, writes home to his family. His letter is sent from Manchester Royal Infirmary, dated the 3rd September 1939. At this point, Tom and Vera have not yet met.

'Dear All
Well, we are 'up and at 'em' at last. We are fully prepared for anything in Manchester. Dozens of barrage balloons, floating gracefully in the sunlight, hospitals evacuated, living in darkness half the time, with windows boarded up and papered to prevent splintering, gas-proof theatres etc.

'I think I will be here for at least nine months – prepared to do casualty work. You need not send my gas mask as I have been provided with a new and better one. You can send me a bottle of whisky if you like! By the way, we are not allowed to phone home as the operator is very much overworked at present. It is really amazing and most encouraging to see how terribly loyal everybody is at the moment, rich and poor alike.

'Hope you are all well and that the corn is safely garnered in - looks as though it might be needed. Give my love to everyone, especially the lads who get called up. If I get called up, I will try to get in the Navy, but I think I shall be stuck here for some time. We have had quite a number of black-out casualties in the last few days – you know, folks celebrating and all that, and then walking into buses in the darkness – coming in with cracked pates and whatnot. Everyone seems extremely confident that old Hitler will 'get his' this time. Even the Poles seem to be shaking him up a bit.

'Hope Dot, Barbara and the 'naughty nippers' had a good holiday. You ought to leave them in Prestatyn. What about Eric? Will he be called up? If so, give me details and give him my very best wishes and tell him to let the b-----s have it good and proper.
Hope Dad isn't getting overworked with his A.R.P. duties.

See you soon – love to all – Tom.'

It was not until July 1992 that Vera wrote her reminiscences for her children and grandchildren and her words begin the story of Vera and Tom, revealing how they came to write their 'Burma letters'.

'We had spent the rather wet afternoon at Montacute House, Janet, Karen and I, and we were on our way home in the car when Karen asked, 'What did Grandpa do in the War, Grandma?' The shutter which had closed my mind for twenty years, since Tommy died, suddenly came apart. I was able to think about him positively.

'This is how we met. It was Christmas Day 1939. It was quiet in the Accident Room in Manchester Royal Infirmary where I was a Staff Nurse on duty. All the drunks from Christmas Eve had been dealt with and sent home. Suddenly the door burst open and in came a dancing, singing group of Housemen who were doing their Christmas tour of the Hospital to entertain the patients. Amongst the group was houseman Tom Ashley. He persuaded me to join the group and, when it went on its way, I went with it. It was love at first sight. Being Christmas, there were parties going on and the whole atmosphere was more relaxed than usual. We met on duty, stole away to the Splint Room to be alone together and met after duty to go to the Rivoli Cinema across the road [6d for nurses]. I had arranged to go to a New Year's party with another houseman. Tommy was working and couldn't go and I could not let my partner down. I think then we realised how much we missed one another. The phones between the Nurses Home and the Residency were very busy as we talked. I could not eat or sleep. I was madly in love – so was Ashy.

'When Ashy died, someone wrote to me and said, 'I had only to see you two together, to know how much you meant to each other'.'

12

Within a week of meeting, their correspondence begins. From the start they use the diminutive 'Ashy' to refer to each other, amused by the fact that their surnames are so similar. Vera's first note to Tom is undated.

'I was perfectly happy until Christmas night. I saw Les on the Tuesday night before Christmas Day and we were terribly happy then and very thrilled because we would be able to spend next Christmas together.

'I was terribly happy on Christmas Night – I can't say why Ashy, because I didn't know you at all - but it was just Heaven to be in your arms – I felt as if I belonged there darling! But after I had said goodbye to you I was absolutely miserable – I couldn't eat or sleep and I just longed to see you.

'Then I began to think I would forget about you, but on New Years Day you were on A.R. for a whole half-day with me. Had you ignored me Ashy, everything would have been alright, but as you insisted on flirting – that was the end as far as I was concerned. Oh darling, I loved you then – even if it was only infatuation, which I think it must be Ashy. But why am I not happy with Les now as I was before? – I hope you will be able to find a solution darling.'

On the first day of the New Year, 1940, Tom writes to Vera,

'Ashy Darling
It is time that you and I stopped to think for a while. Today, New Years Day, has found us both undecided, both wondering what we should do to make ourselves and each other happy. You are officially engaged to a chappie who is, no doubt, very charming, and very much in love with you, and I am unofficially engaged to a girl who is very sweet, unsophisticated and presumably very much in love with me. And yet we both appear to be wondering whether or not we have made a mistake.

'I have known Joyce for nearly eight years now, although it was only a few weeks ago now that I suddenly, on impulse, asked her if she would consider herself engaged to me. When, a few days later, she said yes, I felt at once both happy and strangely uneasy. Perhaps I made a mistake but, if I did, am I not just as likely to make another mistake? And, darling, the same applies to you also. When you became engaged, you must have considered yourself to be in love.

Vera, Staff Nurse

Tom's Graduation

'It is awfully difficult to reason about things like this but we must at least try. Maybe in a few weeks you will think, 'Oh – Ashy is quite good fun and nice to know, but he is terribly selfish, thoughtless and conceited and not worth serious consideration.' I am afraid flirting has become a habit with me. Although I realise that settling down with one girl is the only way to find lasting happiness, I cannot help feeling that if I were not a flirt I should never have known you, and knowing you, in itself, is a source of very real and sincere happiness to me
Yours, 'Ashy'.'

Before the end of January, Tom has broken off his relationship with Joyce. Vera has confessed to Les that she no longer wishes to be engaged to him and she phones Tom to tell him this.

Tom to Vera – undated,

'Ashy Darling
I was ever so glad you rang up last night you have no idea how happy you made me feel. I couldn't tell you on the phone, because I was in the Common Room with all the chaps, but Ashy I do love you, very dearly, and the knowledge that we are both free to start all over again has made me feel like a man looking at a new world, a world full of hope and beauty and you darling.
Yours, Ashy.'

For a while, they both continued to work at the Infirmary and to meet regularly. In May, in common with other medics who 'could not wait to join up', Tom joined the Army and, within a few weeks, he went off to Yorkshire as a Lieutenant in the Royal Army Medical Corps.

In a letter dated 21st May 1940 he mentions that some medics who had been previously trained for war duties were returning from Calais because the town had been bombed. The evacuation of troops from the beaches at Dunkirk was only five days away. No leave is possible because of the escalating situation. Tom is by now stationed in Whitby and he and Vera are desperate to see each other.

He writes, on the 1st June,

'Darling, if you can possibly come here this weekend without rousing the family wrath, I should be terribly happy to see you. You would not have to worry about digs as I could find them for you at a moments notice. I would not ask you only for the fact that I cannot get leave for many weeks to come.'

On the 6th June, Vera writes saying,

'I will let you know definitely if the family will let me come. I must persuade them if I possibly can.'

On annual leave from the Infirmary, she was 'allowed' to spend a weekend in Whitby and she stayed at the Marine Hotel, West Cliff. Only the family knew where she had been for her holiday. Later letters refer to how 'well' they both behaved during this weekend.

The following week, the German army entered Paris and Reynaud resigned as Premier. Petain negotiated an armistice and France became an occupied country.

Vera

On her return to Manchester, Vera writes from the Nurse's home,

'Everyone here was very much upset by the news. It does all seem so hopeless. I know it is selfish, but what seems to hurt now more than anything else is the fact that all this should happen now just when we could be so happy. If we were older and had lived our lives possibly it wouldn't all seem so vital.'

The meeting in Whitby made their desperation to be together even more intense and, by the 16th June, Tom has asked both sets of parents for their approval for them to become engaged to be married.

'I have written to our respective parents and I am expecting their replies in the morning. But, darling, whatever they say, our love for each other will always be as it is now'.

And, two days later,
'Your father has written me a very nice letter and says 'yes'.

However, no response is forthcoming from Fred and Ada. Tom writes to Vera,

'Last night I phoned home and Dad told me to do 'just what I thought I ought to do'. He wasn't annoyed or even just resigned. He said it as though he at last trusted me to make a wise choice.'

Next day, an undated letter from Ada arrives,

'Thanks for the letter and the phone call. We hope you will be very happy son. You don't need telling that and of course you must bring 'Vera' [sic] home when you next get leave. I think Tom, knowing all, as you do, you must understand our seeming reluctance which is only natural to parents [when they have had a great struggle to see a thing through and keep up heads and hearts] that they should dislike the idea of rushing into such a serious thing as marriage for those they love. Also you know our views on the subject. 'Old fashioned,' aren't we? Anyway, here's our love and best wishes to you both and when she meets us she will no doubt understand.'

Tom sends Ada's letter on to Vera, asking her at the same time whether she would be prepared to make her way to the farm to meet Fred and Ada on her own. She replies, on the 21st June,

'I do understand how your Mum and Dad felt about it all, and even now it must be disappointing for them, but I hope I shall be able to make up for their disappointment to some extent, and instead of taking you away from them, I hope I shall be able to make them love me too. I feel dubious about going to see your Mum and Dad alone – but if it would make you feel happier if I went, I will go Ashy.'

Later in the same letter, she writes,

'I had a very sweet letter from Mum and Dad too, hoping that we would be very happy, but they know I'm sure, that I have never been so happy before. We must save these letters then, when we are very old and you have grown your beard, we can recall our memories with them.'

They never were to grow old together although Tom did briefly grow a beard.

Emma writes saying,

'Dad and I are delighted to hear the good news and hope that you and Tommy will be gloriously happy.'

Notice of their engagement appeared in the Manchester Guardian in June and, on the 26th Vera writes,

'Please don't ask me to go to see your parents alone because I should be just horribly scared.' And Tom replies, 'Perhaps you might be right – only it seems such a pity that you should have to wait so long – I do not think I shall get leave for months, unless I get compassionate leave for marriage. Of course, that is not a bad idea, but maybe we had better wait just a few more weeks.'

At this time, their letters mention air-raid warnings taking place almost every night. At the Infirmary, constant practices are put in place for 'Air Raid Precautionary Measures'.

'Today everyone has been walking around half asleep. Last night we had a yellow warning at 1.15am and we were allowed to return to bed at 3am'.

Tom replies, on the 30th,

'We still get plenty of warnings and hear the Jerries passing over nearly every night, but, being British, we take little notice; apprehension turned first to expectation, then to mere speculation and latterly to a state bordering on boredom.' The letter ends, 'Would you be very surprised if I were to suddenly ask you to marry me at very short notice? It is just possible that we will get moved from here shortly, and I may get 48 hours leave, but I cannot say exactly when this is likely to happen.
Happily yours darling, Tom.'

Vera writes back, revealing her concerns about what the families would think,

'I know that we are confident that we wouldn't be making a mistake. I know that we seem to have known and loved each other all our lives and we were just waiting to meet each other, and I know we are sure we shouldn't regret it, but they won't be sure as we are.'

The next day, Tom writes that,

'The unit is packing up to move within 30 miles of Manchester. It is just possible I may get to see you quite soon. We are to be transferred to Huddersfield.'

It begins to seem that they could marry and then return to the occupations to which they both feel so much commitment and, on the 9th July, Tom writes,

'Neither time, space nor Hitler can keep us from each other for very long. I am still laughing at myself and wondering how the careful Tom A. could get into the state where nothing, no-

18

Fred and Ada with Eric, Bessie, Tom and Harold, 1924

one else matters but a single woman. Even my ambitions in medicine are but a part of a life which I want to live for you.
Yours and yours alone, Tom.'

And the next day,

'I want to tell you again that I love you and you only, and if you say yes, neither Matron nor anyone else will be allowed to spoil our plans.'

Her reply comes by return post.

'Just come along very soon and steal me away darling, as soon as you possibly can. It seems futile to wait in case we do have our happiness snatched away. I can't bear to think about that, so let's make sure of it. Oh darling, why should they object? We could be so happy. I do say yes darling.'

And Tom answers,

'I don't want to waste any more time. I am prepared to face the wrath of our parents by marrying you on Saturday next, but if you want to wait a few weeks longer I don't mind – much.'

By the 19th July they have agreed upon a wedding date and Tom writes,

'I am getting terribly impatient darling. The 17th August seems such a long way in the future yet I am so happy. It will take our parents at least a month to get over the shock of it all.'

Emma and Roger, better prepared because Vera had already confided her happiness and anticipation to her mother at least, take the news of an imminent wedding in their stride. During the weekend, the couple visit both sets of parents to discuss the marriage.

Emma is determined to start at once to make plans for the wedding and 'to provide a wedding breakfast', saying, 'It will all be very nice if I have anything to do with it.' She is anxious about Vera meeting Ada and Fred for the first time and writes, 'I hope everyone was kind to you at Tommy's home – I thought about you so many times.'

Tom and Vera go to Oakfield Farm on the 20th July and she meets Fred and Ada for the first time. As well as the speed with which Tom and Vera wish to marry, there are other family undercurrents of which Vera, and possibly Tom, is unaware. The meeting is not a success, and the next day, Tom writes

'It will nearly break my heart getting married without Dad and Mother at the ceremony.'

Fred and Ada loved their son with all their hearts. It is hard today to understand why they would have made him so unhappy as to suggest that they would not go to his wedding. Fred was a strong and stubborn character and he had been brought up in Victorian times when

children did as they were told. Even as an adult, Tom was still under some financial obligation to his family.

Fred was generally kind and gentle but Sunday lunches, when there could be twelve or more members of the family present, were conducted in silence as far as children were concerned. They were told to 'let the meat stop your mouth.' A cuff was quite usual for misdemeanours. However, the powerful sense of the centrality of family life was pervasive at Oakfield Farm; 'up the Moss.' Ada conducted the household and, having come from a home with three older and three younger brothers, she had grown up accustomed to hard work.

Tom was a bright and adored child. He was born at Gerrards Farm, in the bedroom lit by oil lamps, after a long and complicated labour. The delivery was carried out by the family doctor. The priority was to save the mother's life and it was not certain that the boy would survive. Forceps had left marks across his forehead where they had been applied in a desperate attempt to correct the presentation of his little head. Ada, ill and weak, lay awake as Tom 'sobbed and shuddered in his sleep' throughout the night following his birth. That memory never left her.

From about 1918, when the family had moved to Oakfield Farm, Tom attended a small school which was run at Prospect Grange by his Aunts. This school had been opened privately, with the help of Mary Tickle, Fred's Aunt, in 1901. The children were taught by Sarah and Eleanora Ashley [Fred's sisters, who were aged 16 and 14 at the time the school opened.] At eleven, Tom went to Irlam Grammar School and, having done well in Higher School Certificate, he was encouraged to go on to Medical School. However, as he had not done sufficient science or Latin, he had to begin by doing a preliminary course which made the training even longer.

At the time, it was unusual for a farmer's son to have such aspirations. The whole family worked together to enable Tom to go to the University of Manchester. Tom always recognised that Eric in particular made great sacrifices to help his brother; livestock was sold to raise funds. Everyone, including Bessie and Harold, worked to cover the hours of physical work that Tom could not do because he was studying. Life was hard on Barton Moss and cart-horses were still in use with fairly basic agricultural machinery. Farmers were totally dependent on the vagaries of the weather. If there was too much rain, at the wrong time, the boggy ground fought with the farmers to prevent them from making a decent living. In 'good' years, the lush vegetables proliferated and, coaxed from the peaty soil, were sent to London and Manchester for the early morning markets.

Fred and Ada were proud of Tom. Their investment in him was intended to benefit all the family and to provide a buffer against the 'bad' years. This was quite a reasonable assumption. Families were not yet protected by the state against want, poverty and disease. Since the early 19th century the Ashley family had worked hard together to reclaim Barton Moss, to make the land workable and then to build up prize-winning expertise in vegetable production.

Fred and Ada were deeply opposed to a hasty marriage. They had greater ambitions for their son than that, at the start of a war, he should rush into marriage with a young woman from a similarly modest background. Tom was destined to become a surgeon, in his own eyes as well as those of the family, and the road to this would be long, hard and expensive. At that time, such a route also needed 'good' connections. There were other worries and concerns and the threat of war was affecting other members of the family. They had reason to believe that strong passions were not necessarily 'a good thing'. They hoped that Tom would marry 'well' and that he would concentrate on repaying his debt to the family.

Tom never forgot this obligation and, in time, honoured his commitment in full although his career did not take the course he had initially planned.

Tom aged 18

CHAPTER TWO
⇔July 1940 to April 1942⇔

By the 10th July 1940, German planes were bombing English ports and shipping in the Channel. Tom and Vera are due to be married in less than a month. Letters written on the 22nd July cross in the post. It is hard to realise that post went back and forth so rapidly, even if posted quite late in the day, so that their correspondence is like conversation or dialogue in a play.

Vera writes after breakfast, before going on duty at 10 o'clock saying,

'I'm sorry I was so upset last night – I'm sure I made you feel far worse – but I hate the idea of anyone being hurt or worried because we are thoughtless Ashy – we ought to give them time to get used to the idea before we made any definite plans – I don't want to add to their worries.

'I wish they would understand that I love you so deeply that to be without you is just making life pointless, that there is a war which makes everything uncertain, and that even if we were married I would never want you, or allow you, to forget them. I wish they would see that I want them to love me too and that I don't want to take you away from them.'

She suggests writing to Ada herself,

'Do you think if I wrote to your Mum to ask if she would at least come to our wedding she might reconsider it? I feel as if all our happiness was just shattered at our feet -- I think it hurts more than anything else could.
I'll always love you.'

On the same day Tom writes,

'I have been feeling very blue all day and I suppose you too have been rather despondent. It will nearly break my heart getting married without Dad and Mother at the ceremony, but I have written a long letter home today and I hope they will see my point of view and change their minds. Somehow I cannot write much to you now darling but please keep this thought in front of you – I love you more than anything else and I always shall no matter what hardships life holds in store for us.'

By the next day Tom had received Vera's 'beautiful letter'. He responds,

'It is grand of you to face up to things so frankly and bravely. Dad and Mother must be terribly worried about the future when they find it necessary to say they will be unable to come to our wedding. It hurts me to know that Dad and Mum cannot accept my promise that we will never forget them. They seem to think it is wishful thinking on my part when I say that I will be able to send them at least as much when I get married as I can when I am single.

'If Dad and Mum do refuse to come to the wedding it will leave a hurt inside me always but it won't make me feel that I am doing the wrong thing. They have suffered so much in the past and they have so much to worry about in the future that they find themselves unable to understand me – they seem to feel they are being deserted by the son who owes them most and this at a time when they most need his help – a tremendous amount of unhappy feeling has arisen where none need exist.

'Mother is terribly unhappy about it all. You see, she tends to stick up for me, even if she thinks I am wrong, and it is she who has to face Dad when he is annoyed or pessimistic.
I think she would appreciate a letter from you – an understanding letter such as the one I received this morning.'

By the 25th Tom has received a letter from Ada but is still hoping in vain to hear directly from his father.

'However, as nothing is forthcoming, I enclose a letter from Mother – it is a most understanding letter but it shows how much poor Mum is suffering – I still hope that Dad will see our point of view – I am not forgetting my obligation to them – it must be very difficult for Dad in his present position to agree with me.

'I certainly did not foresee all this unhappiness darling – the thought of Dad and/or Mother not being at our wedding is almost unbearable – I know it would make you and your people feel very uncomfortable and unhappy – yet there is no reason why everybody should not be happy about it all.

'It is the most difficult thing in the world to make Dad change his mind once an idea is fixed there and yet I still say that there is hope – I hope to get another letter from home before the weekend.'

Vera writes to Ada - *'because I feel so wretched about her being unhappy.'*

Ada replies,

'Just a few lines to say thank you for your letter and also the invitation to the wedding. I have put off writing thinking I might be able to say 'Yes' for both of us, but it was no use so will you please accept for me alone.

'I hope you are well. I had a letter from Tom this morning and have written to him telling him what I have told you here. I wish it could have been a happier time for us all. There doesn't seem to be anything more I can say. Love A.R. Ashley.'

Although this letter is undated, it must have been received at the end of July – less than three weeks before the planned date for the wedding.

German planes were coming over the east coast and major cities with increasing frequency. On 29th July, after Tom had visited Manchester and returned to Huddersfield, Vera writes,

'I suddenly woke at about 12.30am and heard some planes overhead and then a crash -- a bomb falling near Trafford Park. But as soon as I was awake I thought 'I hope Ashy got back alright because he hadn't got his tin helmet' – I couldn't help laughing when I was awake

because I had thought of you quite without realising it. The bomb did no damage -- it fell near a bridge and shattered the windows of a bank. [I have just realised that this is rather 'careless talk'].'

Their meeting that weekend restores their buoyant mood and confirms their determination to press ahead with their plans. Vera concludes her letter happily,

'I feel so different from last Monday, but why I can't imagine because everything is just the same. Maybe it is because I know we wouldn't be happy without one another. I love you so much darling.'

On the same day, Tom writes to her

'Since seeing you again I am almost my old self and, although I have not yet heard from Dad, I no longer feel miserable. Somehow the trees seem greener, the sky seems more blue and the air smells sweeter than for many days past.'

He concludes,

'I will write to your mother this afternoon darling and send her a list of addresses.'

Only eighteen days before the event is due to take place, it is time to send out the wedding invitations. In a letter of the 31st July Tom begins by saying,

'I was waiting in Stockport Station when the Jerry went over. There were a number of searchlights looking for him and I heard a couple of bangs which I thought were AA gun-fire. However, I arrived back safely at about 2.15 am.'

He shows far more concern, even mild panic, in the rest of the letter referring to the wedding.

'Hope that all the arrangements are proceeding smoothly – if you can think of anything you want me to do please let me know. I am really quite worried lest we forget something important. For instance, I do not yet know exactly where we are to get married and, above all, I must ['remember to' – crossed out] buy a ring.'

There is no sign that Fred is relenting.

'I have not received a letter from home since Friday last so I cannot tell you what Dad is thinking these days'.

Emma has met Vera in town to buy the wedding outfit.

'I have got something quite lovely but I won't tell you what it is. Will you do something for me – I think it is the only thing I want now – will you give me a spray of orchids to wear with it?'

The letters show how tricky it was to organise a speedy wedding when there was a war going on. It was quite uncertain whether or not other close family members would even be able to attend. Tom heard from his younger brother Harold - 'He thinks he will be able to come up for the wedding'.

Later, three days before the wedding, Harold writes to Tom.

'Can you let me know where and when to meet you on Saturday? You'll have to send me a wire. All you need to put is the place and time. If you mention a railway station just mention the town also to avoid any mistakes. Can you find me somewhere to sleep on Saturday night?'

Tom's leave for seven days from the date of the wedding has been approved by the Colonel [but was not actually confirmed until the 13th August]. Vera has not yet arranged her leave from the Hospital with the Matron.

On the 2nd August Tom discovers where the ceremony is to take place when Vera writes,

'I was thrilled to see you are likely to have a week's leave. But darling do you think that Matron will even consider giving me a week? She'll just have to because if she won't I shall just not come back. Will you ring her and ask her Ashy or had I better go and see her?

'We are going to be married at the Congregational Church, Buxton. I don't know the name of the road but it is quite near to the Crescent – I think you'll like it. Don't be worried darling. All I can think of for you to do is to buy a ring, to ring up Matron for me, to think of somewhere to go for a honeymoon and to give me some orchids.'

They see each other briefly in Huddersfield on the 5th August and the next day Vera writes,

'It was grand to come to see you. I have just been thinking how ghastly it would have been if we hadn't ever got to know each other – if I had just gone on being engaged to someone else and if I had never known what happiness I was missing, because I was never really happy before I knew you. With you I am gloriously happy – do you think we shall always feel that way about each other?'

On the 7th she writes to remind Tom to 'write to Matron', who is evidently still in the dark about the wedding plans, and she also asks,

'By the way – shall we have some photographs taken after our wedding? I think we should.'

And luckily, they did. If they had not, whether Fred actually did attend the wedding or whether Tom ever got the orchids might have remained unknown. The flowers prove to be elusive.

'There is some difficulty in obtaining orchids darling. I have been to the best shop in Huddersfield and they will not be able to tell me till Thursday next whether they can obtain any for me – I must visit Dingleys when I come to Manchester -- if anybody can get them they certainly will be able to.'

Tom and Vera
on their Wedding Day

26

Letters cross again as they both write to each other on 11th August. Vera is still concerned that Tom is feeling unhappy about the situation with his father and she agonises about whether they have been unfair to their parents in rushing ahead with the marriage.

'If anything I am more in love than ever. But I'm scared in case this other unhappiness should do something to our love because it could so easily. We have got to convince ourselves that we are right, and I'm afraid that it's not very difficult to be convinced when I'm with you – it's only when I'm alone that I begin to wonder.'

Two practical matters are raised by Vera,

'You should really buy the bridesmaids a present Ashy – a bracelet or something like that. I have written to Mum and asked her to collect something eatable together to take with us on honeymoon. She will know what to get so we needn't bother about that.'

In Tom's letter of the same date he has,

'Completely recovered from the moodiness of last evening and I realise that this was due to self-pity which is really most unjustifiable.'

Writing about the loveliness of the late summer day outside his window he continues,

'Everywhere seems almost as fresh and clean as springtime and you and I have been walking hand in hand through the future, blissfully ignoring obstacles and laughing at mistakes, because from now on darling we have a new motto – 'What must be done, can be done'. Next Saturday will be a changing point -- but it will not change you and me – it must not and therefore cannot.'

There are no more pre-wedding letters from Vera and only two from Tom, one on the 13th August says,

'Have you managed to get seven days off? I do hope so darling. Mother has written to me again. I was very glad to get a letter from her this morning, even though it still seems that Dad has not changed his mind.

'My leave has been approved by the ADMS but as yet no relief has been obtained – I cannot leave here until the Relief Officer has arrived.

'I am not fed up any more because there are two things of which I am very certain
1. I shall always love and remember Dad because he has been such a grand father to me,
2. I shall always love you because you are the only person who can make me really happy.'

And the last one on the 15th August,

'I received a lovely letter from Dad this morning, and his last sentence reads 'I now close wishing you and yours all the best, love from your Dad.'

'You will love him as I do darling when you get to know him. -- I love you so much, Tom'

Tom, Eric and Harold

The next day, the day before the wedding, Vera went home to Buxton. Tom travelled from Huddersfield to be with his family at Oakfield Farm. There is no record of what transpired that evening.

In the wedding photograph the two fathers, Fred and Roger, each with his chin slightly raised, flank the family like book ends. Vera wears flowers, which may be orchids, on the fur collar of her coat.

After the reception at Terry's Corner Café in Buxton they collected the parcel of food put together for them by Emma and went on their honeymoon to Plot 57, Boston Road, Prestatyn. There are no photographs of them while they were away. A picture of the modest wooden chalet with yellow flowers in the open window, two folding chairs either side of the door and a sleeper for a step is remarkably touching. Later letters from Tom in India speak of his passionate longing for that time. The simplicity of their surroundings had been a matter of no importance to them.

The Chalet at Prestatyn

Fred, Ada, Harold, Tom, Vera, Joyce, Emma and Roger & Sheila

Less than a week after the wedding, bombing raids began in earnest in London and by 7th September the Blitz was in progress. Eight days later, on Battle of Britain Day, the British inflicted great damage on the Luftwaffe and Hitler postponed his plans to invade England. In reality there would have been little to stop him from breaking through and Tom and Vera might have been living in a country under Nazi rule.

Instead, they returned from their honeymoon to go back to their jobs in Manchester and Huddersfield and the letters resume for they were to remain apart for a while longer. Some letters from Vera appear to be missing from this series.

On the 25th September Tom writes,

'It was marvellous to hear your voice again yesterday. You sounded so happy and near to me. – Last evening I was so tired that I fell asleep immediately after dinner and did not waken until 10.30 – just in time to hear planes overhead and a little later I heard some bombs drop a few miles away.

'I hope your rest has not been disturbed, darling, because you too must be still tired. - It was all so marvellous that I shall never forget one minute of it. It all seems like a dream still and I think it will always appear so because everything was so grand and crazily happy. – How shall I close – 'Your loving husband', 'eternally yours, dear wife' or just 'Cheerio darling'? All my love, Tom.'

As soon as he gets back to Huddersfield, Tom becomes involved in a concentrated programme of inoculating and medically examining men in military training. He must have received a letter from Vera which crosses with his because he writes,

'Your letter was just as I had hoped it would be telling me that you are happy, telling me that you loved me and missed me and yet full of confidence in the future. – I will meet you at 2.45 on Wednesday as arranged.'

They seem only to have met for the day, and Tom writes,

'I think I shall be able to get to Manchester on Sunday but, as there have been raids on this district, I shall have to get permission from the adjutant. I am looking forward ever so much to seeing you on Saturday, but even more to October 18th when we can really begin to live together as we want to.

'Speaking to you on the phone this afternoon – we both seemed to forget the war and sleepless nights --I felt as though you and I were apart from it all, and that our little world was something remote from worry, something that can never be broken up and destroyed – I know that we can build a little world of our own to live in. – It amazes me to find how much I philosophise and dream these days, how much my whole life is filled with but one thought – 'How can I keep my Ashy as happy as she is now?'

On his return to Huddersfield, Tom found a promising house for them to rent. More and more men were being inoculated and vaccinated, the Officers in Huddersfield had been called out during the night to 'stand-to' and all leave had been stopped. On the 10th September Tom has evidently received a letter from Vera and he replies,

'Your news, although as you say, not really surprising, is indeed a subject for serious thought, but not, I hope, a cause for worry. You ask me what you should do darling and in reply all I can say is - do nothing, but just go on living and laughing as though everything was just as usual. After all it is really too early yet for you to know definitely that it might not be a temporary upset in the normal routine.'

Vera is very unwell with a throat infection and all leave remains stopped so they are not together again until the end of the month and Tom writes on the 30th September,

'I have felt so miserable since you went that I almost feel as though I am going to have a baby myself! When I think of the strain you are suffering now darling it makes me feel very small and selfish and yet I cannot help feeling strangely happy inside me.

'My thoughts are with you all day darling and I do hope that you can overcome this unpleasant feeling in the mornings. – I have decided to 'take you for a walk' every morning at 6.45am – tomorrow we will start by going hand-in-hand to Corbar Hill along the road towards the reservoir and then up to the left along the side of the wood until we come to a small hollow in the ground where we will just lie in the sun until breakfast is over and you vanish over the horizon leaving your husband still loving you and waiting for you to return.'

On the 1st October Vera has *'received some most lovely roses from the grandest, sweetest person in the world.'*

They go for more 'walks' together. One day Tom takes her to Solomon's Temple in Buxton and the next to Oakfield Farm on Irlam Moss, where

'The creeper on the house will now be a vivid mass of colour and the bracken in the woods will all be turning brown and will crackle under our feet as we walk, and it will be great for watching startled hares and cock-pheasants popping out of the undergrowth as we stroll along, until we eventually find a sheltered corner where we can sit on the crunchy bracken and just dream about the lovely things in the world.'

On the same day Vera takes Tom for a walk that they had done together in Prestatyn and,

'At the top of the hill we sat down and watched the sea and saw a glorious view. Everything was quiet and peaceful and cool and the roses were out. We walked up the hill again this morning Ashy and you held my hand tightly'

She was suffering badly from early morning sickness but,

'I thought hard about you and it was really amazing because I had some breakfast and felt perfectly alright – not sick at all.'

The evening before, Vera and a friend had been to the Gaumont Cinema to see Hitchcock's 'Rebecca'which they found 'simply grand'. They had what she described as 'a lively time'.

'While we were there the sirens went. We stayed until the picture was over and then we walked back. All the time we could hear planes overhead and then some bombs and gunfire so we sheltered by the University and then made a dash for the Hospital. There was quite a lot of damage done. An incendiary bomb was dropped just inside Lister House gates. It didn't do any damage except to the cabbages but Withington was hit right and left.

'The White Lion and the Scala Picture House were bombed, an air-raid shelter was hit and garages, shops and houses. They dropped incendiary bombs near the Christie Hospital. We had about eight casualties here. Altogether they had a hectic time – they are still getting bodies out of the debris. It was certainly a night and a half. Sophie and I went to sleep in the air raid shelter and stayed there until 6.30am – so I was late for our walk after all today darling. Don't worry about me darling, just love me and think about me will you? I love you more than anything in the world.'

Tom replies,

'You seem to be having some entertainment in Manchester! I guessed that it had been bombed when I read in the papers that an 'inland north-west town' had been visited by Jerry, so you can guess how glad I was to get your letter. – I think we will go to that little stream by the Church near the Manchester Grammar School sport's ground tomorrow and just lean against the railings and look at the moon through the trees. Remember?'

On the 9th October Vera writes, mentioning what was later revealed as quite a premonition.

'The gun-fire is terrific. We keep having visions of the out-patient building falling on top of us – we are in the dispensing shelter tonight. Last night Rusty and I went to the Opera House to see 'Iolanthe'. It was awfully good and the singing was glorious. – Just as we were coming out the sirens went.'

They join forces with some other colleagues from the Hospital including some male medics.

'They escorted us back and walked up the corridor with us where we were seen by the Home Sister. She recognised me and told Sister Jackson who ticked me off wholesale today for 'encouraging men to loiter on the corridors.' – The gunfire still continues and it is almost 10pm now. We were sure there wouldn't be a warning tonight because it is pouring with rain and very dark. – I'm beginning to feel very sleepy so I think I'll say goodnight.'

For all the understatement of their letters, anxiety must have run high. Tom writes,

'I was so glad to receive two letters from you – yesterday I had no letters and I knew that Jerry had been over Manchester again - I hope you managed to get back to the Royal Infirmary before the fireworks started. Don't stay out too late at nights will you darling? When you get this letter you will be able to say 'A week tomorrow I go to Ashy' and you will know I am thinking the same.'

On the night of the 11th/12th October 1940 such a serious raid takes place on the Nurses Home that Vera sends a telegram,

'New Home' hit. All safe. Ring me tonight – love Vera.'

Later in the year, a newspaper report of the damage in the Manchester Guardian [although the cutting is undated] was published.

'The Hospital needs to appeal for special war donations to avert or reduce the deficit of nearly £20,000 with which it is threatened; in the hope that friends and supporters may be tempted to push their hands in their pockets to support an institution whose staff show such an admirable devotion to duty.

'During a raid the Nurses' Home suffered a direct hit from a high explosive bomb which penetrated the roof and exploded in the great hall a few feet from an air raid shelter under the main corridor. One hundred and twelve nurses were in the shelter in bed in the bunks. – Some of the nurses were covered with soil and dirt. At the same time, water – from broken pipes poured into the shelter. The nurses maintained perfect order and made their way out to the Infirmary – where they received attention, many of them being covered with dirt, wet through and clothed only in their night clothes. Apart from severe shock, they were none of them injured in any way in spite of masses of broken glass and other wreckage. The great hall and the recreation rooms at each end were completely destroyed. -- The bomb pierced the roof and struck a twelve inch girder, which it bent to such an extent that the girder measured some two feet more than its original size. The bomb exploded in the ceiling of the great hall. Had it gone to the floor and pierced the foundations both severe loss of life and damage to the structure must have occurred.'

Vera was covered in dirt and wet through but she was safe - and so was her baby.

Tom evidently came to Manchester the next day, and the air raids continued unabated, because on the 14th he writes,

'I hope you arrived back safely before the air raid last night. We were still in the station when the gun-fire started. I looked at my watch as the noise began and noted that it was 20 minutes since you had left me, and I had visions of you sprinting the last 100 yards with shrapnel falling left and right. I bet you swore!

'It was marvellous being with you yesterday darling and I don't think I shall ever forget the fun we had, especially the crazy episode in the shelter. It was grand to see Mum and Dad looking so happy and to know that they love you Ashy but then I always knew they would. I was up at 7am today in good time to hold a skin inspection of 160 men before 8.45.'

On the 15th of October Vera is to move to Huddersfield and has only three more nights to spend at the infirmary.

'It was grand to see you – everything is quite different when you come – bombs and direct hits and things like that just don't exist any more.'

Tom writes two letters which end this series.

'I inspected another 150 men before 9am and I have another 200 more to see in the morning. I am getting this job over and done with before you come! It will be so marvellous to have you here darling. I will be outside the station at 6 o'clock just in case you are early.'

They were to spend fifteen months together in Huddersfield and, many years later, Vera reminisced about this time.

'We rented a furnished house and lived happily there. It had a nice garden overlooking a small valley. There was lots of social life- it was strange at first meeting brigadiers and colonels and their wives – but one soon learned to fit in with army life. The colonel was rather randy and used to pinch my bottom given the opportunity.

'Meanwhile, Tommy became a captain attached to Signals. We used to dress up for evening engagements and I had two lovely evening dresses – one was in navy taffeta trimmed with

cream lace. It was very elegant, with shoe-string shoulder straps.

'Janet was born on the 13th May 1941 at the Princess Mary Nursing Home. She was a pretty pink and white baby with golden hair and she was our pride and joy. We were invited to a sherry party by the Brigadier and he tucked a bottle of sherry beside her in her pram.'

During June, Vera stays with Emma and Roger. The weather is very hot and Tom writes about his garden.

'It's doing marvellously well with this sun – even the strawberries are taking shape.' The letter ends, 'Look after yourself darling and take good care of my baby.'

Janet

Tom goes away on a scheme and his letters show how keen he is on physical activity, swimming and playing squash at every opportunity. He mentions, with relish, the quantity of roast and fried food he consumes, with special reference to fried breakfasts every day, and 'I also managed to get 20 Players No. 3.' A letter from Tom on 26 June mentions Janet's Christening which is to take place on the following Sunday.

'Laurie Liversedge, who tells me he gave up being a 'conchie about 12 months ago, is to be Godfather and Dad and Mum are both coming too so we shall have quite a party'.

Letters from Tom to Vera, who was in Buxton with Janet during October, suggest that she had gone home to Emma and Roger for a while because she was ill and tired. There is a later reference in a letter from Vera to her having suffered from 'nervous exhaustion'.

Vera and Janet

Harold, Tom and Eric

Vera said in her reminiscences which she later wrote for the family,

'Always in the background was the knowledge that the war was going on and that inevitably Ashy would be posted overseas. Somehow we lived from day to day and tried not to think of the future. We had a Christmas tree for Janet's first Christmas and she had lots of soft toys.'

During this waiting period, Tom and Vera also spent time 'up the Moss' with his family. A photograph shows Vera, laughing, wearing Tom's greatcoat and hat on the front lawn at Oakfields. Other members of the family lived nearby and they enjoyed the company of Bessie and Laurie with their three children, Sheila, Teddy and David and also that of Eric and Dot with their sons Tony and Bill. Harold still lived at home on the farm; Barbara, their foster-sister, helped out with the band of cousins. The lives of all of them were to be disrupted by the war.

Vera remembered,

'In April 1942, Tom was posted to Crookham before going overseas. He landed in Bombay and was posted to various places in India, and then to Burma where the war with Japan was at its height. Jan and I moved in to 22 Overdale Avenue. They could not have found it easy to have their retirement invaded by us but we were made very welcome in their small house and they never complained. If I had not had Janet, who I loved with all my heart and my life centred round her, I would have joined the Forces. Instead, I joined the Women's Voluntary Service and did a little nursing.'

Roger and Emma would have done anything for their daughters. Emma, in particular, was very concerned about illness and proper care and rest. Antibiotics were still a thing of the future and she and Roger had an all too tragic reason to fear disease. Vera remembered the way in which Emma looked after her after Tom left.

'Foolishly I insisted on seeing him off from Stockport Station. It was horrid and I was so upset that I caught the wrong train and found myself in Manchester instead of in Buxton. Over the next few weeks, I missed Ashy so much that I lost pounds in weight and looked like a skeleton. However, I was looked after by my mother and gradually recovered.'

Vera had almost certainly been on the verge of anorexia but Emma's care enabled her to recover. Emma was a natural homemaker and carer. To stay with her as a grandchild was to feel safe and cherished and to believe that all would be well.

Roger and Emma had known each other for many years before they were able to marry. He grew up living at Highfield House in Tideswell and his father was a fierce disciplinarian – to the extent that Roger was very unhappy during his childhood. Roger left home at the age of 21 to join 'the Northampton Borough Police as Constable, on the 20th September 1900 and he resigned his situation as Sergeant on the 21st October 1925 during which time his conduct was 'Exemplary'.

Emma Slack grew up as part of a large family who had a successful retail business in Tideswell. She and Roger eventually married on the 3rd September 1907 at 8am in Tideswell Church when they were both aged twenty seven. They moved to a small terraced house in Cyril Street, Northampton. Their son, Frederick Evans Ashton was born in 1908.

He died at home in his mother's arms, aged six, of peritonitis caused by a perforated appendix.

Emma was terrified of the idea of having another child because her first delivery had been such a dreadful experience. She once described how all her children 'had to be gained' which was taken to mean a forceps delivery. However, 'Roger begged her to have another child'. In 1917, Vera was born and in 1921, when Emma was aged forty, Joyce.

Roger, Emma, Vera and Joyce, 1924

Vera spent her early years very happily in Northampton and she was sad when, in 1925, the family moved to New Farm in Tideswell. She left behind good friends and her much loved Convent School. New Farm was a dismal, isolated building but Emma quickly made it into a comfortable home and Vera did well at Lady Manner's School. The winters were very hard; and Roger developed diabetes. Following a winter in which Joyce was extremely ill, they moved to 22 Overdale Avenue, a new house in Buxton, and Vera began her nurse training at the Manchester Royal Infirmary.

Vera, 1933

37

Vera in
Tom's greatcoat

Eric and Dot
and Bessie and Laurie

Vera and Joyce

Barbara with
Tony, Sheila, Bill, Teddy and David

CHAPTER THREE

≈1942≈

1942 was a year of defeat and retreat in Europe and in South East Asia.

In December 1941 the Japanese attacked the naval base at Pearl Harbor and reactions to this were of 'stunned surprise.' Lord Ismay wrote,

'It had never occurred to anyone in London, nor do I believe in Washington, that such a thing was possible. The initial response of the British government was to feel relieved and thankful because the Americans would become allies and ultimate victory would be certain. However, our Eastern possessions, almost undefended, were now open to the Japanese. My optimism would have been mitigated if I had known the fearful losses which had been suffered by the United States Navy, or realised the cataract of disaster that lay ahead of us.'

[Ismay.1960. P241]

Discussions in Washington led to 'decisions of the highest consequence,' one being 'that the elimination of Germany should be our primary objective' [Ismay. 1960. P243] The United States and Britain together declared war upon Japan and the Japanese went on the offensive in Burma, Malaya and the Philippine Islands.

'Within a week of Pearl Harbor, the Japanese had burst into Burma, for Burma forms the natural strategic shield of their conquests in the South-West Pacific.'

[Owen. HMSO. 1946. P11]

The Battle of Burma took place and, on a day in February 1942, under immense pressure, men of the 17th Indian Division were 'retreating along the coast of Burma towards Rangoon.' Lieutenant-Colonel Owen writes that, 'the men were ordered to retire beyond the Sittang, the third and last moat between the Japanese invaders and Rangoon, main British base in Burma.' By dusk the sappers had decked a bridge to allow the retreating troops to cross the river with their vehicles and equipment and; 'the stream of vehicles bearing wounded, stores and rations begins to cross the river. All down the track, as the leading files start off, exhausted soldiers drag themselves out of the ruts where they have dozed as they stood. An army of sleepwalkers moves towards the bridge.'

Men and equipment crossed the river during the night but, at daybreak, the Japanese came in from the north and blocked the road to the bridge. There was massive fighting and confusion.

'The fog of war wrapped itself about the struggle on the Sittang. – Four hours after midnight, the most dreaded possibility of all threatened to become a fact: the bridge might fall. If it did, two Japanese divisions would drive straight on to Rangoon.' The decision was taken to destroy the bridge leaving many men stranded. Some managed to cross by swimming and by pushing wounded comrades on logs or bamboo rafts.

'Our casualties were double those of the enemy and the moral effect of the disaster on the Sittang was as damaging as the physical losses.' However, the Japanese were crucially delayed. In March when they eventually reached Rangoon, the port had been methodically evacuated and destroyed. The British forces had been able to withdraw, regroup and to liaise with the Chinese.

'The shattered units of the Sittang lived to fight many another day. – They would arrive at last on the mountain frontier of India, battered but unbroken and still fighting on their feet, bearing their weapons and their wounded. And then, out of this remnant of a rearguard would rise once more an unconquerable army.'

[Owen.HMSO.1946.P 7-10]

'On 15 February 1942, Singapore surrendered unconditionally. Speaking in the House of Commons, Churchill called it 'the greatest disaster to British arms which our history records'. On 8 March, Java followed suit. Almost simultaneously Rangoon was abandoned and Burma lay open to the invader. – The Japanese had complete command of the Bay of Bengal, and both India and Ceylon lay wide open to attack. In India itself, political agitation inspired by Gandhi had led to serious internal uprising. No-one had ever expected that retribution for our unpreparedness in the Far East would be so swift or so catastrophic.'

[Ismay.Heinemann.1960.P247]

'The outstanding and incontrovertible fact was that we had taken a thorough beating. We, the Allies, had been outmanoeuvred, outfought and outgeneralled. The first and overriding one was lack of preparation – no higher authority had expected an invasion of Burma.'

[Slim.Cassell.1956.P115]

The Army of Burma was forced into inexorable retreat, their battle was lost and, by the end of May, 'all the land of Burma passed to Japan'.

[Owen.HMSO.1946 P24]

Tom arrived in India just as the monsoon broke in 1942 and, towards the end of June, he came into contact with this tattered band. The first time and only time he writes about it is in a letter to his parents, in June 1945, telling them what he had encountered.

'I was stationed in Fyzabad for two months. One of my jobs then was 'snooping' and I first went up to Manipur Road. On this trip I met many refugees from Burma – senior army officers, half-caste Anglo-Burmans, Indian peasants, forestry officials, battered British, Indian and Chinese soldiers; walking skeletons, suffering and dying from cholera, dysentery, typhus, malaria, heat exhaustion and starvation. I saw Dimapur, a hell on earth, reeking with the damp smell of jungle at its densest, full of mosquitoes carrying the death-producing, malignant malaria parasite; I saw Manipur Road – the beginning of the way back.

'The Manipur Road then was rough and single track and thousands of coolies from the tea gardens were swarming like ants over the craggy hills of Manipur, tearing at the hills, digging, picking, carrying, levelling, sweating to make the road wider and safer. The pioneer company I took up went straight onto the job with their picks and shovels and baskets, and I went back to Fyzabad, realising for the first time the meaning and the magnitude of war.'

In January 1942, Tom's preparation to go 'overseas' begins in earnest and he goes to Edinburgh on a training course. In February he is in London staying at the District Transit Camp and attending the London School of Tropical Medicine. On the 23rd, the lectures are on-

'Plague and cholera, from the great Manson-Baker – he is a fine lecturer and told us one or two good stories. The lectures are very full and contain a mass of detail as the course should really last two months and we are trying to learn it all in 14 days.'

By February, Kuala Lumpur and Singapore have fallen to the Japanese and Australia is threatened when Darwin is bombed on February 19th.

Tom goes to Hampshire early in April and on the 7th writes from Boyce Barracks in Crookham.

'This is a queer sort of a place, a straggling village outside Aldershot apparently serving mainly as a depot for the RAMC officers and men. Our billets are not bad and the mess is quite nice – the food is good in quality and well cooked but sadly deficient in quantity so far as the Manchester lads are concerned.'

Rumours circulate, but they still do not know their ultimate destination. Meanwhile, Vera and Janet have begun their 'Buxton' lives with Emma and Roger. Vera has seen Tom off on the train to Hampshire and she returns to Buxton in a very distressed state. She knows she will not see Tom again before he sails, they have very little chance to speak on the phone, and no idea of how long their separation will last. Tom tries to keep the tone of his letters light.

'Your Mum really is marvellous the way she has taken you two scamps under her wing without so much as a grumble. I shall have to bring her a parrot or a monkey to replace you both when I come back to reclaim you.'

He concludes the same letter, written on the 9th April, with what he ruefully describes as 'one of my celebrated lectures'.

'a] You must not worry if at any time my letters should cease to arrive. The question of secrecy may forbid me from writing from certain places and a long sea voyage would inevitably mean that I shall not be able to write for days or even weeks.
b] Never believe rumours about anything.
c] Don't forget that I will miss you just as much as you miss me.
d] Don't ever fall out of love with me no matter how long it may be before I come back.
e] Don't let Janet forget me.
f] Keep yourselves fit and well for me.

I love you, darling – Tom.'

On the 11th he writes thanking Vera for sending some 'snaps' and says,

'Isn't it a pity that I didn't have one taken with Janet, but still men look so soft holding babies that it is perhaps just as well that we didn't take one.'

Tom with Janet

However, a photograph of Tom 'together' with Janet, aged about eight months, *does* exist.

In the same letter, he says,

'We will not be staying here much longer. I will not be able to tell you when or from where we are to sail darling, but I shall be able to write to you just before we set off for distant lands. If and when we call in at a port we will be able to send cables home, providing we keep absolute secrecy about routes. If you should ever make a guess – you must keep it absolutely secret.

'I am going to keep a diary of the trip and I hope that you will keep one too so that we can compare notes later. It will be fun tracing Janet's evolution. I wonder what she will be like when she starts walking and talking. Let me know about all the little changes.'

Vera replies,

'I won't let Janet forget you darling. She says 'night-night' to you every night when she goes to bed. It has been glorious weather here. Corbar Woods and Solomon's Temple look very inviting – but not for me on my own. For me, at the moment, they are more inviting just as a memory.'

An undated letter from Tom is the first of a series of ten letters written at sea. It must be the one he posted as his ship left port.

'My Darling,
Until we meet again we must concentrate our thoughts on happy memories of the past and hopes of the future. Afternoons in Out Patients, evenings by a little stream in Wythenshawe and days strolling through the woods to Solomon's Temple or up Corbar Hill; sherry at Christmas time, the fascinating charm of our Jan, the fun of being at 59 and the possibilities of happy holidays in France, America or Blackpool, the thrill of opening my first surgery and of teaching Jan to be a lovely lady.

'All these thoughts and many more must crowd our minds to the exclusion of all thoughts of parting and war. The present must be lived for its own sake. I must play my part in this wretched war and you must play your part at home. We have no alternative because the present does not belong to us. But the past and the future are ours darling and we must continue to live them in our thoughts.

'When I come back darling you will find that I have not changed. I will feel content that I have played my part and Prestatyn will again see the smiling faces of two young people very much in love with each other. All my love to you both – Tom.'

Vera replies on the 25th, and it was probably weeks before Tom receives this letter as he was 'somewhere in the Atlantic' on the 23rd and had been at sea 'for many days'. From now on, the letters assume quite a different character because they cease to take the form of dialogue. They are all the more moving because of the revelation of their passionate hopes and fears which would not receive a response for weeks at a time.

Vera reveals her thoughts as Tom recedes from her to an unknown destination,

'I received a letter from you but where it came from I can't imagine. I'm doing my best to be philosophical about all this upheaval but it's not easy to readjust oneself all at once. In time I shall be able to realise that all this had to be – I know we couldn't go on as we were – even though we were very happy, there was always the feeling behind it all that it couldn't last and that one day something would come to shatter out peace and happiness.

'Don't worry darling, I'm gradually settling down and Jan is just marvellous. She's such a loving little darling. She puts her arms round my neck and snuggles up to be loved. But you can't wonder at it, can you Ashy?'

During the long sea voyage which was to last from mid-April until the 5thJune, Tom wants to share every experience. He writes ten letters and at first he says, 'I will number them all,' however this does not turn out to be practical.

The second letter, written 'at sea' on 23rd April, says,

'The sea is dead calm – it's quite hot but not yet unbearable. You would love to see the sea in these parts. It is a wonderful inky blue in colour and as the wash swirls away from the ship it turns light green. At night you can see hundreds of phosphorescent particles of living plankton which sparkle when disturbed and brought into contact with the air – at night it is like a girdle of stars in the sea around the circumference of the ship.

'The food is really marvellous and cigarettes and tobacco are plentiful and cheap and we can have as much chocolate as we like. Our day's routine is quite varied and interesting and we have no time to get bored or become morbid. – We have little time to sit and think because we all have a great deal of reading to get through. This is very fortunate because thought inevitably leads to home, and thoughts of home with you and Jan, darling, inevitably leads to worry and self-torture but these we must overcome somehow.

'On Tuesday 21st at 8pm I went to my bunk to rest -- and for a few moments I felt you very close to me darling – I was sure that you were reading my last letter and thinking of me sailing away, but suddenly you vanished and I couldn't recall you. You often seem to be right by my side. I wouldn't be at all surprised to meet you and Jan sometime when I turn around. – Time will seem to pass quickly in the next few months with so much about to happen in the world.'

They were not to know then that the months would become years.

By the 28th, Tom can see,

'A brilliant three-quarter moon in a clear sky and we can see the Southern Cross. – For the last few days we have amused ourselves by watching flying fish, of which I have now seen many scores, they really are remarkable.'

On the 4th May, the convoy puts into port 'for a few days, but we were not allowed to land or to send cables.' Soon after this port of call Tom reports that they are drinking 'South African champagne' on board ship.

Tom has received no mail from Vera and is very keen to know if she is 'fit' and had gained some weight.

'The last few evenings have been glorious darling and I have missed you terribly. The moon has been full and I could plainly see The Plough, Orion and the Southern Cross. I did wish you were with me. One night in particular the moon was very lovely and I sat for about an hour on the boat-deck thinking of home.

'An amazing chain of thoughts passed through my mind. I saw quite clearly things which happened when I was 5 or 6 years old and I metaphorically shook hands with dozens of my old friends and so on through my school days, University and the Manchester Royal Infirmary to Whitby, Prestatyn, Buxton and Huddersfield. I couldn't help thinking about what a lucky fellow I have been and, apart from leaving you and Janet darling, there are very few phases of my life that I would not care to live over again – certainly nothing in the last two years. Those were happy days darling and they will come again.

'We had a heavy rainstorm a few days ago. It was marvellous to rush up to the top-deck for a freshwater shower – normally we have to content ourselves with salt-water bath so this warm, torrential rain was much appreciated. At the same time, we availed ourselves of the opportunity of washing our linen. You would have been very amused to see dozens of officers, young and old, naked and semi-naked, scrubbing shirts and pyjamas on the top-deck and revelling in the rain like a lot of school-boys.'

Tom adds to the letter,

'The weather has changed and it's much cooler today. The fresh breeze and lovely blue sky bring to my mind very much pictures of the beauty of England in May – I am glad that Janet was born in May. She seems to 'fit in' so beautifully.'

In the same letter, the war comes into sharp focus as Tom mentions the 'Baedeker' raids, so named because the attacks were upon historic English towns that are described in German guidebooks.

'We occasionally hear news from London and we were very thrilled to hear about the British landing on Madagascar, but we were distressed to hear about the new series of German 'hate raids' on old English towns. I can't see what good these will do the Jerry. No doubt the RAF chaps are giving him far more than he bargained for. Our confidence in ultimate victory never weakens. I have seen some encouraging signs of the British and allied war effort which I cannot talk about now.

'I particularly love to sit and dream on the top deck at night, either alone or talking with friends. We have so much in common. Our love for old England and our desire to do our bit are prevalent thoughts and all three of us have left loved ones at home. – I like two chaps much more than the rest of the crowd; Johnson, - a typical public school boy and Lipacombe who was born in Sydney and came to practice in England 10 years ago'

'It's strange but we all three feel very strongly that this trip is not really part of our lives. We are not in the least resentful. We all realise that what we are doing, though not of our own choosing, is yet something which has to be done and done by us, but all the time our spiritual life goes on at home with our wives and families and friends. It is only our bodies that have left all we love at home in order that we may live freely again.'

On the 13th May Tom writes,

'Today our Janet is one year old. How I wish that I were at home so that we could have a party. I am having a little birthday party on board ship this evening in honour of Jan. My cabin mates and I will share a couple of bottles of wine [South African Champagne 11/6d a bottle] and will then play bridge or go on deck to look at the stars and reminisce about days gone by.'

Later, 'we celebrated Janet's birthday – I had her photograph with me and we all signed our names on the back. The chaps think she is marvellous.'

By the 17th, they are in port and disembark for the first time on the voyage. Although 'I cannot yet give you details of the sights I have seen' - it is evident that the port is Cape Town. He writes to describe the brief time they spent there,

'We have just left one of the word's most beautiful cities, and we will all bring away with us very happy memories. On the day we reached port, I rose early and was on deck at 6.30 and was one of the first to see land – a range of mountains rising to a great height in the distant sea and mingling with the heavy grey sky. At seven I saw a great, yellow, blinding sun rise clear of the biggest and most majestic of the mountain tops. It was a truly grand spectacle.

'Slowly we steamed into port, picking out first trees and then houses in the mountain sides and, by 9am we could plainly see the town itself nestling close to the foot of the mountains and extending down to the sea. The town seemed to make a complete crescent, filling in the shore all around the semi-circular bay. The houses, mainly white or cream with red roofs, looked very clean and beautiful set in this lovely green bay with a background of most inspiring hills, which latter were now overhung by a thin film of cloud.'

They are made extremely welcome by the residents who offer unstinting hospitality. A dance has been organised for that evening despite the fact that,

'No-one had expected us in until we had actually been seen entering the bay. I was very lucky and met a charming family who entertained me like a long lost son. They had me out for tea and dinner on more than one occasion and they took me round in their car to see local beauty spots and to swim – if only they could have produced you and Jan. How I wish we could come here and live one day. It's a beautiful and rich country, grand people, wonderful climate and a thousand and one interesting things to do. Unfortunately there is no room for 'foreign' doctors.'

Almost 60 years later, at that point quite unknowingly, Janet saw the same sights and probably walked past the house of the family with whom Tom had stayed at Newlands.

He asks Vera to,

'Have a really good, large portrait of you and Jan taken to send when I know where I am to be stationed. – I miss you and wish desperately that this war will end soon in order that we can get together again, go to see the beautiful things in life together again and to talk and laugh together again. Some day, we will darling.'

Letters 8 and 9 are written as the voyage is coming to a close and their tone is lyrical, passionate and sad. He describes 'a most majestic dawn' over the Indian Ocean.

'The sun quickly rose clear of the sea and shone for a few moments in all its red-gold glory before disappearing behind a black cloud, leaving behind a pool of gold which merged into orange and red along the band of sky between cloud and horizon. At the same time radiant beams appeared above the cloud, making the upper edge silver first directly above the sun and then spreading slowly, peripherally like a creeping silver snake. Soon the sun rose above the cloud; the cloud which was black became white and the sea which was grey became silver and the sky which was grey became blue and my thoughts which were also grey became green, green with envy and love for England in May, Buxton in May, Corbar in May. Remember, darling?

'The night before last I began to sleep under the stars, slung in a hammock and rocking gently in the breeze. For a long while I could not sleep. The night was so lovely, the moon and stars so bright and my thoughts of you so vivid.'

Later, he was resting on his bunk when the music steward put 'Starlight Serenade' on the gramophone and,

'You came right to me. My imagination was so startlingly clear that I wanted to cry. Instead I went for a bath, lest my friends should see how upset I was.'

Tom describes how, at the moment that he steps into the water, he remembers Vera gently lowering their baby into her bath. His words are infinitely tender and the image of Tom's tears and his own vulnerable, naked body is powerfully evoked.

'Empire Day' was followed by Whit Monday so the men celebrate over a long weekend.

'In our cabin we drank a little Empire Hock but others imbibed more potent fluids and we were greatly entertained until quite a late hour. The next day the merrymakers are still cheerful. On deck, they met at the for'ard starboard corner. This, they say, is New Brighton. How beautiful the lighthouse looks with the waves smashing against the rocks at its base and the sands crowded with happy holiday makers. Then a wag says, 'Away lads, let's go to Southport.' And we all hike laughingly across the deck to the for'ard port corner to see racing motorists on that long stretch of beach, to see the hundreds of bathing belles in the pool, to sail our model yachts on the pond.

'And so we amuse ourselves; fighting boredom, fighting depression and yet not terribly unhappy because we know that love, like England, is steadfast and can outlive this war and the war cannot go on for ever.'

By the 1st June, they are steadily approaching their destination and letters 9 and 10 end this series.

'I have not written to you for a whole week, and yet you have been more close to me this week than at any time since leaving home. Sleeping under the stars seems to give us more in common and I find it easier to visualise you and Janet. I see you doing all sorts of things from walking down a moonbeam to sleeping on the settee at home. Two evenings last week, I listened to the men singing on the troop decks. They sang many songs including 'Two Eyes of Blue'. This was very moving but the eyes I saw were not blue darling. On Sunday we were given a piano recital by one of the men. He played beautifully. Strange to think that someday his beautiful hands will manipulate a weapon of war.

'I wonder if you have received any of my letters and how many you have written to me. It seems years since I heard from you. Soon we will be able to send each other Aerographs and news will be speedily exchanged in comparison with the present. How is our little darling?'We have had lectures almost daily. These have dealt mainly with Tropical Diseases and have been given by members of the draft – some have been very interesting, some boring and some of no value whatsoever. Last week I gave one on the 'History of Indian Medicine' - strange to relate, this was well-received probably more because of its brevity than interest value. I am reading 'The Surgery of Modern Warfare' by Hamilton Bailey – very interesting. I'm reading quite widely and I am amazed at my own ignorance of the world in general and our Empire in particular.'

He goes on to say, that 'this trip may prove of value in different ways.

' 1] I am presumably a necessary, infinitely small part in a very big machine.
2] The experiences through which I am passing are not only widening my knowledge but also broadening my outlook on the Army in particular and man in general.
3] Last, but by no means least, I do feel that you will have a chance to regain your health.

'I miss you terribly at times. All day long I miss the little things. A million thoughts will keep me company always darling and, with so much of our lives ahead of us, we must think only of the ten million happy moments to come. This war is only a brief interlude and until it is won we could never fully live the life that you and I want to live. Your letters will mean so much to me.'

On the 5th June the men are 'busily engaged in packing our valises and trunks.' The temperature is 97 degrees in the shade and 'in the lower parts of the ship must be 130 degrees.' This is the last letter written 'at sea'. They hope to be 'going to hospitals for a while' when they land.

'This would buck me up no end as I feel very rusty in my clinical work. We are all tired of filling in time with lectures and reading and are anxious to get down to some real work. I can hardly believe we have been on this ship for such a long time, life has seemed very beautiful and I have wished that you could be with me to see so much; but I still think that life has nothing more beautiful to offer than a day on the green hills of England – you know where and when.'

Tom disembarked from the Orbita on the 8th June and he reported to the Office of the DQ [Rail], Ballard Pier, Alexander Docks, Bombay. From there he went by Punjab Mail train from the Victoria Terminus to the British Military Hospital Fyzabad, India and his first letter from there is written on the 16th.

A letter from 'Bing', sent from Murree, Punjab, dated 24th July 1942 mentions 'returning a book' to Tom. It mentions 'our original party of 4' being 'split up'. 'Lipo' was in Abbocabad and 'Johnnie' was in Rawalpindi. He 'sighs for a party of the Orbita calibre', so this is likely to be the ship they sailed out on from the Clyde. They all signed their names on the back of the photo on Janet's birthday.

It is not until the 4th July that Tom receives letters from England.

'A few days ago I got your first letters – I wonder if you can realise how much they meant to me darling. You really are marvellous Ashy. When I come home again, life will start again, and it will start just where it stopped on April 7th. Nothing can change us sweetheart.'

Vera's letters are written and sent into a void as she does not receive any communication from Tom until the beginning of June. From 30th April she writes about Janet's development and about everyday events, which were not startling, in Buxton. Every week, Vera goes with friends or Emma or Joyce to the Cinema and also to concerts or plays at the Pavilion Gardens and the Playhouse.

'Janet has grown amazingly; her hair is definitely ginger and her eyes bluer. She pulls funny faces – screws up her nose and winks both eyes at once. I have to laugh although I suppose I should take no notice. She has no idea of walking at all.'

Vera tells about friends and relatives visiting and about going to the 'flicks' or for long walks.

'Sophie came and we went for a walk to Corbar Woods. I thought about you darling – at least about two unknown people who were so madly carefree and happy there. Do you remember them?'

The letter gives further insight into Vera's state of health.

'I often think about George Avenue Ashy. Do you remember how fed up I was this time last year – especially when you and Marjorie fired the chimney. I must have been desperately tired for a long time darling because now I never lose my temper with Janet and I used to so often. It was queer because I always adored her. So please forgive me Ashy. When you come back I hope you will find a very sweet-tempered wife and a darling daughter who are very good pals.'

She mentions having suffered from 'nervous debility' some time after Janet's birth and also, in a later letter,

'I had a letter last week from John Platt written on his way to India. He was very fed up and, much to my surprise, he said how much he envied our having Janet. Are you surprised Ashy? I seemed, before Jan was born, to have a queer sort of complex that everyone thought it crazy to have babies in wartime. It rather upset me somehow and I didn't look forward to her arrival as I know I otherwise would.'

Vera mentions joining the Tennis Club in Ashwood Park and she sometimes does some nursing. This is intermittent and part-time. Income Tax was 10 shillings [50p] in the pound so the financial rewards were slight.

'It seems very odd writing to you each week and yet not hearing from you. I'm just living to hear from you at the moment. Sometimes I wonder if I really have a husband or if he was just a dream, but looking at Janet makes me sure I must have a husband somewhere around. The view from my bedroom window is lovely Ashy. I can see a rolling sea of trees with spires and domes showing between. It's a lovely sight especially at night when I can see it lying in bed and it is getting dusk and everything looks misty and shadowy. I feel as if you are here then darling looking at all the loveliness with me.'

Like Tom, Vera found certain melodies on the wireless, in shows or films almost unbearably poignant.

'At a variety show where they played 'There'll always be an England' I wanted to run away and just think about you.'

On the 7th June Vera receives the letter Tom wrote early in the voyage, and also a cable which he probably sent from Cape Town, and she replies

'It worried me not to be able to imagine what you were doing and who you were with but now I have a lovely picture of it all. I suppose you have arrived by now – according to the wireless and the papers a large convoy has arrived safely without loss.

'Life goes on here the same as usual. The weather has been simply marvellous this week and Janet has worn just her dress and pants. She is quite brown. I think I will send her to you by air-mail for a few lessons in good behaviour. She is no longer the docile sweet-tempered child we knew – she is a little monkey who shrieks at the top of her voice, clambers all over me, eats the heads off buttercups and daisies when she gets the chance, crawls into the kitchen and picks up the cat's milk and tips it down herself and gets as black and as dirty as she possibly can. But she's a darling and what I would do without her I don't know.'

Everyday items are in short supply and often rationed. All sources of food have to be carefully conserved and Emma is expert in this field. In August, Vera writes,

'We have been making jam and bottling fruit until we look like it here. There have been piles of blackcurrants, redcurrants, raspberries and gooseberries in the garden this year. We had quite a few strawberries too so we are well-supplied for the winter. We have had lots of peas and tiny beetroots.'

It is Joyce's 21st birthday in June and a party is held at 22 Overdale Avenue. About 14 people sit down for tea.

'We had a glorious tea considering there is a war on. The cake was super – I would love to send you some. We had a tongue which Mum had saved for ages – mixed fruit, strawberries and cream [tinned], salad with tomatoes and all sorts of cakes.

'I've been watching Janet when she is playing. Dad fished out the old toy box we had when we were kids. You would be amazed at the queer assortment of things we have collected. There is a box of very grubby bricks but she is very fond of them and she can build six one on top of the other. There are several books of 'moo-cows' all rather tattered and torn but great favourites. There's a little red leather bag, into which she stuffs all sorts of things, an old watch, a top, several bottles with or without tops, a ball, a little rubber cat, a powder tin, a rattle, a doll and several other odds and ends. We keep it under the kitchen table. Janet comes along and pulls it out and strews everything all over the floor.'

In his letter of the 7th, Tom says how close to her he has been feeling, and she replies,

'It was queer I should be so near to you one night Ashy, because do you know I was feeling absolutely heartbroken on that particular night and you came right here beside me. It was absolutely amazing because you seemed to be really here, telling me not to cry just as you always did and I felt much happier and have done ever since. It was so strange. I thought I must be dreaming but I was wide awake.

'When do you think you will really be home again? I keep thinking how marvellous it will be when you come back. Every time I go to the station I think of the day I'll be going to meet you. It wouldn't be so bad if I could say definitely that it will be a year or even two.'

Checking stores

Vera writes weekly throughout the summer, keeping Tom in touch with life at home. She is doing some part-time nursing and leaving Janet with Emma.

'She seems to be thriving on it and Mum doesn't seem to mind – but then she never minds anything – she is such a darling. If my daughter, when she grows up, behaves as her daughter does now, at times, I think I shall spank her. But Mum never seems to get perturbed.

'I'm surer than ever that you must have reached your destination now because it said on the wireless this morning that the Duke of Gloucester had arrived in India and that he left England in early April.'

By the 12th June, Vera has received a cable from India giving Tom's address. She writes, telling him about the seasons, the beautiful weather, visits to see the family and, as promised, how Janet is developing.

'She is quite tall now Ashy and full of mischief. You would laugh if you had seen her the other night. She was in the big bath. I had washed her hair and we were splashing and playing. Then Janet hung onto the side of the bath and stood up and peeped over at me. Her hair was all wet and flat against her head and honestly Ashy she looked exactly like you. I was absolutely amazed at the likeness. She got an extra hug and a kiss that night.

'Tonight I saw Tom Ashley looking at me from a pair of bright baby eyes under some damp gingery curls. I got such a thrill, but it often happens and every day I love Janet more and more – not only because she reminds me so much of you darling but because she is so sweet and so lovely. I often just look at her and wonder but I know I have no reason to wonder because she is just our love personified.

'I do hope our letters are arriving by now. It would be rather a good idea to keep them because my diary is full of spaces so far. I think these letters would be far better than any diary.'

In July, Vera and Janet go 'up the Moss' to stay with Ada and Fred. She conjures up a clear picture of home for Tom,

'It seems very queer being here without you and everywhere seems very empty. Everywhere is looking lovely. The corn is tall and you can see it over the top of the garden hedge. They are busy with lettuce now of course. Everything is so green – the hedges, the fields and the creeper over the house. The garden is ablaze in front of it all. There is a lovely wisteria by the door – it is a dark clover shade. The rambler is out all over the archway and all the roses are out too. There are some very dark blue delphiniums and blazing marigolds and nasturtiums in the background. The pear trees seem to be full; the apples not so good and there have been a few cherries and piles of gooseberries. Am I making your mouth water darling? I've no idea what you eat out there.

'Janet is very sweet and they all love her here. She laughs all day long and is full of beans. Cousins Tony and Bill are well and I wish you could see Janet with them. They will have fun when they get older. They bring their toys out for her and she bounces around on her bottom laughing and shouting and making as much noise as they.

'She's very loveable and loving too. She always gives me a kiss when she comes into my bed in the mornings. The other morning I suddenly remembered I had been dreaming about you Ashy. It had been so marvellous and I was feeling so sorry it was only a dream. I'm sure she knew because she suddenly planted a kiss right on my lips. Won't it be fun when she can walk and talk and we shall be so lively that the time will fly by until the marvellous day we shall be dashing to the station to meet you and then we shall all live happily ever after.'

The visit to the farm seems to have been a success.

'I have got to know your family better – just how sweet and considerate your Mum is – your Dad, I still don't know. He's always nice, and is very fond of Janet, but he always seems distant. Bess is happier now, not grumbling as she usually does. I like Dot more than I have before. We are going to Prestatyn in the middle of August if I can pluck up sufficient courage to go without you sweetheart. I'm so terribly scared of being hurt and upset all over again just when I have got myself more or less settled down again – so far as I will be settled until you come home.

'My feelings are steeled against almost any attack now. Not so long ago a letter or music on the wireless would even upset me, but now I'm more or less immune. How Prestatyn would affect me I don't know. Don't imagine I'm unhappy darling – just having Janet makes that impossible and most of the day we laugh and have great fun together. Being here at the farm seems to have settled me considerably Ashy because you still live here.

'We had our photograph taken together and I'll let you have it as soon as possible.'

By August, Tom and Vera are in touch by cable and aerogram but letters take much longer to arrive. A letter written by Tom on the 18th June, and numbered 11, is received on the 1st August in Buxton.

'It came by airmail and took at least a fortnight less than your other letters. Some must be long overdue because the last one I received was marked '5'.'

Tom's letter tells about his 38 hour journey from the port of disembarkation to Fyzabad and about the climate which is between 110 and 120 degrees each day – 'the worst time of the whole year.'

'The country really is amazing. At the moment, the land is quite parched, the cattle are starving, everything and everyone is waiting and praying for the rains which are due in a week or so now – people work silently and patiently, waiting and waiting.'

He is comfortable in a pleasant bungalow with congenial colleagues and,

'An elderly bearer with a beard; he does everything for me. Morning tea, bath, laundry, clothes, shopping, feeding – all are cared for. He's a grand old boy. I'll send you a photograph.'

Tom is in charge of a medical ward with Indian patients and, although needing an interpreter initially, he quickly begins to learn sufficient words in several dialects in order to 'examine a patient and understand him well enough to make a diagnosis.' He also mentions a photo that Vera had sent to him of herself in Tom's greatcoat.

Vera responds,

'I can see you will be requiring a personal valet when you come home darling. A mere wife will be incapable of dealing with your demands! Isn't the snap of me in your greatcoat priceless? I had forgotten all about it. I bet you roared with laughing. I certainly look quite merry and bright considering that my heart was slowly breaking when it was taken. I think I could stand almost anything after the absolute agony of that week before you went. But I have settled down now, just living for the day when you will be here again, ticking me off and loving me.

'I have got the proofs of the photos we had taken at Lafayette's and they are super – they are 2 guineas for three – I'll let you have one as soon as possible.

'I didn't know how you are faring for news and reading, so I have arranged for Smiths' to send you the Manchester Guardian Weekly and some magazines. We've seen 'Next of Kin' – you know the 'careless talk' propaganda film. It was very impressive and I wish you could

have seen it. You should be very fit playing tennis and swimming regularly – I do envy you. Have you everything you want darling in the way of shirts, shorts etc? Please let me know if there's anything I can send you. It looks like being a perfect bank holiday weekend. It's really hot today. It will soon be two years since we were married Ashy. Couldn't we put the clock back for two years just for August 17th? Oh darling, if only we could.'

Tom sends more photographs. Despite his view that men 'look soppy with babies' he had done something about the lack of a photo of him together with Janet.

'I hope you will like the one of Janet and I – clever isn't it? Do I look like a loving Daddy?'

Snaps of 'Tarzan' and Sidiq are also enclosed. Although the longed-for rains had come, Tom is swimming, boating and cycling several times a week.

Tom as Tarzan

'You'll think I never do any work! I am not overwhelmed, although on some days life is pretty hectic. Most of my cases are suffering from malaria – some have dysentery and a few are pneumonia or meningitis cases. The language problem is very amusing at times. For instance, a patient may be a Malayan - he will probably speak Tamil or Madrasi; another patient will speak Madrasi and Urdu, and the Anglo-Indian nurses speak Urdu and English – so we all stand around the bed and I endeavour to elicit symptoms! Fortunately many of the patients are very intelligent and so we get on reasonably well. A few days ago I got your first letters. I wonder if you can realise how much they meant to me darling.'

He leaves Fyzabad on the 19th August and is directed 'to proceed to Meerut and to report to O.C., 14C.C.S. there for duty by 20th August 1942. He is to serve with the 14 Casualty Clearing Station.

'I am a general Duty Officer and lorry driver. I feel much happier and more settled in this unit. We are all young officers and we feel we can pull together and make this C.C.S. into one of the best in India.'

It is not until he sends a letter to Fred and Ada in June 1945 that more details emerge about this episode. Censorship would have made it impossible for him to share the locations in the letters he wrote at the time.

'In August I joined the CCS, and after two months I was back in Dimapur – we stayed there for five days in torrential rain, 10% of our men caught malaria and then we moved off over the mountains to Imphal, over mountains more rugged and high than the Highlands of Scotland, winding up and up, getting dizzy just watching the pebbles on the road and the millions of bamboo trees on the hill-slopes, skidding perilously round hair-pin bends with a sheer drop of hundreds of feet only two feet from the edge of the road, not conscious of any danger, only thrilling to the knowledge that, at last, we were going in to do a job.'

Tom describes the meticulous work of thousands of men working on what became the crucial Ledo Road.

'Widening, levelling, patiently removing landslides, building bridges and buttressing to prevent further land slips. No-one at home has any idea of the magnitude of the task which confronted our engineers on this road.'

Tom writes to Vera on the 6th September saying he is 'on the road' and,
'From now on we have only the beauties of nature to please us and the pests of nature to annoy us. One need not seek for either. Unfortunately the latter predominate.' He was concerned about letters and photographs possibly being lost. 'Aerograms are always welcome Ashy but it is the letters that really bring you to me darling. They are so much more personal and everything you tell me is so clear and easy to visualise.'

He resumes writing several days later.
'I suddenly realised that I was not sufficiently cheerful to write home – we were in a jungle and the climate was damp and oppressive and had a noticeable affect on one's outlook and temper. But now, we have passed on through beautiful mountain country with glorious tree-covered slopes and waterfalls and blue skies with fleecy clouds and fresh cold air, and we are settling down in a very pleasant station with hills all around and green trees and grass around us everywhere.'

He is heartened to receive a large quantity of mail including letters from Vera, family and friends and magazines and newspapers, saying,
'It was really wonderful to receive such a marvellous mail when I was least expecting it, and your letters Ashy are so grand. One was nearly four months old, but I will read it again and again until I know it by heart. You were at Oakfield when you started it and you finished it in Buxton. In it you tell me all about our lovely Janet in her bath and about your feelings towards all at Oakfield. I am so glad that you were happy there. You must be spending a small fortune on magazines and newspapers! Rest assured they are greatly appreciated by all the members of the Mess. – They are not easy to obtain up here – Luckily we bought a wireless before we left and it is a great boon. We can pick up London easily on the Short Wave. We can always pick up the news – 1pm your time, 7.30pm our time. Tonight we heard that Tobruk had been re-taken. With all the exciting news from North Africa we can hardly leave the wireless alone.'

Montgomery had taken charge of the Eighth Army in North Africa in August and the Battle of El Alamein was fought in October 1942. Tom ends this letter,
'After the war we will buy a house on a hill and we'll call it 'Corbar Hill'. I think we'll both know just what we want from life and will be happy setting out to get it. What do we want Ashy? My answer is a happy family – I wonder what yours is?'

Letters written in September and October 1942 indicate that the men are training and working together to prepare themselves for action and Tom's letter of June 1945 reveals more about this phase than he was able to say at the time.

'We opened our first casualty clearing station two miles beyond Imphal and for us began a period of hard work, which has gone on almost without rest until the present time. Within three days of putting our first tent on the field we had admitted 300 patients – mostly malaria

Tom, before and after having dysentery

Tom with his friends from the village

and dysentery cases. All the troops [and engineers] pass through 'the green hell of the Kabaw valley'; as Slim describes it 'The Kabaw Valley, well-termed Death Valley on account of its virulent malaria.'

To Vera, in 1942 he can only say;
'Here there is much that is interesting and much that is beautiful. The more interesting things are not suitable for discussion in war-time letters.' He takes part in some surgical procedures and he ends a letter on 18th October,

'We are very proud of this unit, we feel that it is ours, and despite the hard work, we are all still as keen as mustard. - I now consider myself to be a reasonably efficient Quarter Master. Perhaps, someday soon, we will find that we will have as much medicine and surgery as we could wish for, possibly even too much. I am hoping that I will be detailed for duties as anaesthetist and assistant surgeon.'

In November 1942, the Allied forces land in Morocco and Algeria in Operation Torch. The Russians cut off the German forces in Stalingrad and the approach of Christmas makes Tom and Vera lonely and nostalgic.

As Tom writes he is 'thinking of Christmas' – remembering those of the previous three years,
'Memories we have in thousands, all beautiful and precious, hope is undaunted and inspired anew by our present successes in Libya and by the heroic defenders of Stalingrad. And here, although hard days lie ahead, everyone is confident of victory, and the feeling is growing that the day is not far off when the end of this wretched war will come in view. Mail from you to me and from me to you may be delayed for a time.

'I hope that this winter will not be too hard for you all. No doubt old Lord Woolton [Minister for Food] will do his job well again. It will be great fun to receive a parcel from you darling. I do wish you could put some of your Mum's fruit cake in and then squeeze yourself and Jan into a corner and send it off by registered air mail.'

Vera and Janet, 1942

Meanwhile, in Buxton,
'Mum has bought a Christmas tree and Dad has put it into a pot so it's all ready to be decorated. Come and help us sweetheart. I shall miss you so much. I'm scared I shall be terribly homesick for you and all the memories that Christmas always brings. But never mind, perhaps the war will soon be over and you'll be home again Ashy. I can hardly believe how glorious it will be. How I shall show off my daughter – our daughter- for your benefit. All my letters are, as far as Jan is concerned, 'from Daddy.'

Just before Christmas, Tom receives the studio portrait of Vera and Janet.

'My first reaction of pleasure and pride was only momentary, to be replaced by a bitterness and selfish hatred of all the circumstances which have driven me away from you and our lovely Jan. I wanted to cry, I wanted to go out and hit somebody, anybody. I lost interest in my work and did only such things as I had to do. You will hardly believe how intense ones feelings are in this climate.'

He goes on to say that 'this mood did not last' but, nevertheless, his commanding officer told him to take ten days leave. 'At short notice I packed up and left for Calcutta.' While on leave, Tom took the opportunity to travel to see friends.

'36 hours travelling there – 24 unforgettable hours spent with old friends – and then 36 hours rush back to Calcutta. 24 hours of real happiness Ashy, just like old times. On my first day in Calcutta I bought a frame for the photograph and it stands on the table by my bed. The temporary feeling of hatred has gone to be replaced by one of inevitability, but the emotions of pleasure and pride have returned. How can I feel otherwise, with such positive evidence that I am the luckiest fellow in the world? My Ashy and our Janet – how I want to hug them both. As I write this letter, I am eight and a half months nearer to them than I was when we said 'good-bye.'

Tom with an elephant

Their final letters for the year reflect the longing they feel for each other at Christmas time. Vera describes every detail of their day in Buxton.

'I love the snaps you sent us darling. We roared with laughter at the one of you in a turban. Oh darling I do wish you were here to tell me all about it. How did you spend Christmas sweetheart? I wonder if you received your parcel. I wish you could have been here on Christmas morning. Of course, Jan had all the presents this time – you should have seen her face as we undid parcel after parcel. She had about eight books.

'One of the books has pictures of ordinary things such as apples, aeroplanes, dogs, cats etc. and Jan knows most of them. I was so thrilled because the first time she saw it she told me the names of lots of them. I did up my old cradle with a pillow and eiderdown and yesterday she was putting her doll in and covering it up and then she would take it out again and say 'What's the matter dolly?' She's starting to put words together now.

'I love you Ashy and I miss you frightfully. When do you think the war will be over? Forgive this crazy letter sweetheart. I don't seem to be able to get my thoughts together tonight. Write often and always love me. Look after yourself.'

Tom with a turban

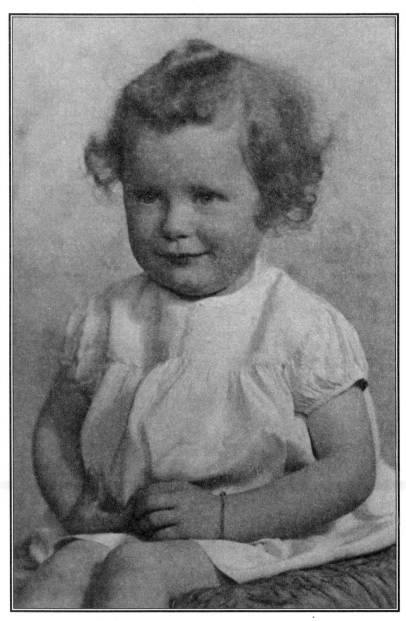

Janet, 1943

CHAPTER FOUR

≈1943≈

Following the retreat from Burma into India in 1942, morale was generally low, and, during 1943, military action was virtually on hold in India. The allies had agreed that,

'The elimination of Germany should be our primary objective, and that Japan should be contained until that had been achieved.' [Ismay.1960. P243]

William Slim, Commander of the Fourteenth Army, knew that,

'We had to beat Germany first. I was even ready to accept that the 14th Army was the Cinderella of all the British armies, and we would only get what her richer sisters in Africa and Europe could spare. I would not grumble too much if we came last for men, tanks, guns and the rest, but I would protest, and never cease from protesting, that we should be at the bottom of the list for medical aid. That was not fair, nor do I believe wise.'

[Slim. 1956. P177]

Slim recognised the crucial need to maintain morale and to gain some measure of control over the appalling toll that was being inflicted upon the troops by disease. Apart from the difficulties with supplies,

'My second great problem was health. –for every man evacuated with wounds we had 124 evacuated sick.' Malaria, dysentery, typhus and skin diseases were the main problems. 'The sick rate of men evacuated from their units rose to over twelve per thousand per day. A simple calculation told me that in a matter of months at this rate my army would have melted away. We had to stop men going sick, or if they went sick, from staying sick. We tackled this on four main lines:
1] The application of the latest medical research.
2] The treatment of the sick in forward areas.
3] The air evacuation of serious casualties.
4] The raising of morale.' [Slim. 1956. Pp177 - 183]

Tom's role, throughout 1943, was concerned with the maintenance of the health of the men. His first few letters are cheerful and hopeful but later in the year he becomes dispirited about the lack of progress with the Burma Campaign and his spirits plummet.

Tom writes to Vera on 3rd January – her 26th birthday. He wants to know all about their Christmas in Buxton.

'Tell me about all the presents and cards you both received. Tell me who you saw and what you did and thought, tell me all about Janet's misbehaviours and tricks. How are Mum and

Dad and Joyce keeping? I bet they all tried to make everything seem just as in the days of peace.

'It is good to hear the news these days, everywhere we seem to be holding our own and building up and fighting back – the Russians are putting up a grand show and we are all cheered by the continued good news from North Africa. Soon we may expect mail by the Mediterranean and then letters will only take half as long as they take via the Cape – just fancy darling, all our little letters travelling 10 to 15 thousand miles before they are delivered.

'It's grand to receive parcels – the socks you made are marvellous – by the way you should include a list of everything you send because parcels sometimes get opened en route – the best thing to do is to stitch the parcel up in muslin and to seal with a sealing iron. Parcels are great fun but not nearly so good as receiving long, long letters Ashy. I must close now as it is bedtime – 11.30 here and 6pm at home, you will just be finishing your tea. I love you - all my love to you both, Ashy.'

Vera's letters constantly ask Tom whether he is fit and thinking of home and what he is actually doing. On the 9th January he gives a sketch of his day.

'You keep asking me what I am doing and how I am. Well, I am very fit and getting fat. I wake at 6.45 every morning, have tea in bed, light a cigarette and think of you. After breakfast I struggle across to the ward. I have dysenteries, venereal diseases, chicken pox, mumps, malarias and convalescents to look after – not to mention scabies and ringworms. I am still anaesthetist and assistant surgeon – this work I do on another ward as and when required. I am doing quite a lot of minor surgery – abscesses, piles, ulcers and fractures. I have assisted with a few 'abdominals' and two days ago I actually opened an abdomen again to find an abscess that we drained and closed up again. The same day I gave a couple of spinals with my usual first time skill!

'After lunch, rest and plenty of tea in the middle of the day we do final dressings, supervise the 5pm medicine round, and fill up returns and records and by 6.30pm I retire to my tent for a well-earned hot bath – in my little green canvas square bath. From eight to ten pm is spent in the Mess for dinner and after that, we do our night round, make our entries in the night report book and generally retire to our couches at about 11.30pm. I light a last cigarette and dream – always in the dream there is a lovely lady who means so much to me.'

A little later in January, he sends a pencil sketch of the Officer's Mess,

'which is made of a bamboo framework over which is plastered river mud, the roof is thatched and the result is quite a pleasant little bungalow with sitting room, dining room and kitchen. We are really quite comfortable here. Excellent food is provided, always followed by the inevitable, ever-welcome cup of tea – as you see darling, we do ourselves very well and we all seem to be putting on weight. The climate here is certainly very much to my liking. It is a pleasant change to huddle round a fire at night. By mid-day it is quite hot again and we go around in shorts and shirts.'

Several long letters written in January and February seem to indicate that, although he is busy, Tom has a certain amount of leisure and is in very good spirits. He takes time to describe the different tribes and castes from which the 'men' come, indicating his admiration in particular for the Sikhs from the Punjab and Ghurkhas from the free state of Nepal. He talks about his batman, Kalloo, who 'is a Mohammedan with bandy legs and lovely teeth'. He tells about the extraordinary number of uses to which bamboo can be put, including 'building scaffolding around the Taj Mahal.'

He wonders all the time about how Janet is growing and developing and one letter reveals that it was more by luck than judgement that she had been born at all.

Janet

'I am so glad that you find her such fun Ashy. Does it ever occur to you to think how strange it was that we neither of us stopped to think, to argue as to why we should or why we should not have a little Jan? I am glad now that we just didn't stop to think.

'I love to read your descriptions of our Jan, what she looks like, the clothes she wears, the antics she gets up to, but it is very difficult for me to imagine what she really looks like. I am sure that I shall have to be very careful how I approach her when I get back. No doubt she will be so much in love with her Mummy that it will take me years to win even a little of her affection! Or do you think I might be as lucky with her as I was with Vera Ashton!

'A few days ago we had the local Maharajah to dine with us and after dinner we were given a show by his best dancing girls – the technique is much different from ours but it is quite attractive – you need not worry, they have a bodyguard.

'The other night I heard 'Destiny Waltz' on the wireless whilst I was having dinner, so you and I danced all over the table, round the soup plates, in and out of the cruet, over the Colonel's napkin and finally we sat down in the old chair by the fire at number 59. Oh yes, Ashy, we still have some fun together, but there are times when I miss you terribly.'

In February, Tom sends 'snaps' and his letters include detailed descriptions of the surrounding countryside, animal and bird life.

'I wish I had a shot-gun with me because there are thousands of duck and snipe out here.'

Tom always made friends readily and sought out new experiences.

'The villagers in this part of India are very friendly and I often chat with them – I also have quite a large out-patient clinic; an old man from one of the villages brings me new cases every day. Getting to know these villagers is my most interesting hobby these days.' And a month later, he reports,

'I am still getting a number of patients from the local villages. I seem to have cured all the old man's cases but now an old lady brings me new ones. At the moment, I am treating two sweet little girls aged 4 and 5. One has a boil under her left eye and the other has impetigo. They come up daily for treatment – they never complain and they smile shyly when I talk to them. The people here tell me that our medicines and ointments are very good. Sometimes the old people bring me oranges and they lend us spade and bamboo cutting tools when we require them.' His friendship with the villagers led to an extraordinary dance display on one of their religious festivals and he writes a long letter describing this.

'We are still having pleasant weather with occasional thunderstorms that threaten to wash us away but by trenching around them we manage to keep snug and dry. I like tent life very much and really am feeling very fit, but sometimes I miss you terribly and it hurts like hell to think you may be feeling the same, and that we can do absolutely nothing about it except stop grumbling and get on with the job.'

Mail seems to have been much delayed because Vera did not have a letter from Tom between Christmas and March 3rd and, on that date, she 'takes him on a walk with Janet across the Common'.

'It was a lovely afternoon. You could feel spring in the air and everywhere looked green even though it is only March. It was beautifully fresh over the Common. Lots of people were playing golf and out walking. We cut across the golf course and so I let Janet walk over the grass. We had to stop and look over walls at ducks and hens and particularly at two cats asleep on some hay in the sun. They intrigued her immensely and when we got back she said to Mum, 'two pussies asleep.'

'She loved running on the grass, her face glowed with the fresh air and her hair shone in the sun, and I loved her, darling, with all my heart and wished with all my heart too that you could see her and hear her saying 'Look Mummy, look Mummy.' You would have looked at her with love in your eyes too darling. Then we came home and had a huge tea, played with dolls and cradles and bricks and looked at books until it was 6.15pm and bath-time, bed-time and a tired little girl was tucked up for the night, saying her prayers and kissing her Daddy's photo goodnight.'

These words, conjuring up images that may seem sentimental today, must have meant everything to Tom and, later that month, Vera writes again when she has received his letters telling her about the conditions in their camp.

'I have learned so much about you from your letters Ashy – so much that I wanted to know and my picture of you is much more alive than it was possible for it to be before. Thank you for the sketch of the Mess. I'll stick it in our album. The result of my labours is really quite good. I have started off with some snaps of me aged about four and continued through School, New Farm, Huddersfield and Buxton and a few of Irlam and then the ones you sent from India. It serves to bring back very happy memories sweetheart.'

An old green photograph album is part of the source material for this book.

'I'll always remember darling and I'll always love you. You are always here with Jan and me – nothing we do excludes you sweetheart and always at bedtime we think about you. I'm just living for the moment when I shall see you again, be in your arms again and really see and

Tom reading a letter from Vera

feel you – not just imagine it. It's rather amazing what faith and hope it is possible to produce when you have to because otherwise how drab and pointless life would be when the person you love more than anything in the world is miles away. I wondered often how the arrival of our photographs would affect you. I knew it would upset you darling and I didn't want it to. I wanted it to bring Jan and me to you and most of all I wanted you to know how sweet your daughter is. However, I am happy if you are proud of it now.'

There is a hint of just how well Vera is being looked after by Emma.

'When Mum brings our tea in the mornings she always brings the post, if there is any. Janet – in my bed by this time – looks on the tray and, if there are no letters, says in a disappointed voice, 'No post!' But, if there is a letter, she bounces up and down nearly knocking the tea over, yelling 'Letter from Daddy, letter from Daddy!'

'I have asked Syd to get me a 'Go-chair'. I want a light chair for her now and here they are a minus quantity but we saw lots in Halifax. I think I shall sell the big pram then, darling, because they are scarce and we have nowhere to store it here.
'I think Jan talks very well Ashy. If I'm cross with her she puts her arms around my neck and her cheek against mine and says' Solly Mummy.' She knows perfectly well I can't be cross with her after that - could you Ashy, if you saw two baby blue eyes gazing at you hopefully and a little mouth saying 'Solly'. Of course, I pick her up and hug her and we usually end up dancing around the room.'

It is Tom's birthday on the 8th April and Vera finishes her letter, quite light-heartedly,

'How does my husband feel now he is 30 years old? I suppose he feels very ancient, or says he does.'

On almost the same date, Tom is writing,

'Sometimes I find it hard to believe that I have a daughter Ashy, but I know only too well that I have a wife and that she is thousands of miles away from me. It is hellish at times. I wonder if we can ever recapture the old carefree happiness. As you say, we will both be older when the war ends – goodness knows how much older, but we mustn't let it make any difference. Despite the responsibility of bringing up a family and earning a living we must somehow try to get back to the spirit of our early time together. Knowing that such happiness is possible, and that it is denied to one makes life seem pretty grim at times but, at the same time, darling, it gives one courage and keeps something inside one living and hoping.

'If only I could hear your voice or see you smile, or hold your hand, for just a few minutes each day life would be so much different. In another six days it will be twelve months since that awful day when I had to leave you standing alone on Stockport Station – 365 days of happiness missed and never to be had again, and yet sweetheart I still feel I am one of the luckiest men in the world. Memory of happiness is the next best thing to happiness itself, and hoping for further happiness to come is another way of keeping cheerful and trying to keep young.'

At the end of April, great gains had been made in Europe but the war in India was still largely a holding operation and Tom's mood is sad and reflective.

'Oh Ashy darling, some moments are still so near and clear to me that I almost want to speak aloud to you; in fact I sometimes do at night. I wish that you could really be near to me again, just once in a little while.

'Life out here seems so unnatural, so illusory. Everyone one meets is unreal, we are all acting, pretending to be this, pretending to be that, trying to pretend to be good soldiers and not really knowing how, not happy, not miserable, laughing easily, eating well, playing and working hard, showing little outward sign that life is abnormal, but if only everyone in the world could simultaneously stand still, and stop for a moment and think, I wonder if this stupid war would last for another day.

'If only we could all, with one voice, say what bloody fools we are, why don't we go home and live and love with the ones who need us and whom we need? But the people will not stop, they cannot stop – the illusion must continue – the war must be won. Perhaps it is the instinctive knowledge of this inevitability that prevents the people from stopping and thinking and going quietly home.
'Going quietly home, going quietly home – how lovely a thought Ashy.'

Both Tom and Vera found consolation and peace in contemplating nature and the countryside. Throughout their letters, it is a recurring theme in their memories of the early days of their relationship. In May, Tom writes,

'I am sitting at table waiting for breakfast and looking across the meadows to the tree-covered hills. It is already quite warm. I am in short-sleeves – and the mist around the hills suggests that it will be hot again today. On the roof is an old crow croaking, in the trees a number of birds are calling and over the meadows larks are climbing and carolling. On the meadow itself is a large herd of cows with many little calves.

'There is a feeling of Spring in the air, somewhat reminiscent of a certain day in Buxton, only here the grass is not such a brilliant green, there are no men in white flannel trousers chasing a little red ball, there is no brass band, there is no you – only the feeling is here, the knowledge that this is nature, these things are beautiful and real and incapable of complete destruction, and maybe you are looking and listening to nature and thinking with me.'

Later in the same month, Tom has received several letters and it seems that there is real optimism about the progress of the war. Vera writes in mid-April,

'The news is grand these days, isn't it darling? – North Africa, Russia and bombing by the RAF and Americans all over the place. If only it would be over soon. When the war in the West is over, don't doubt that I shall come to see you.'

Tom replies,

'It is grand to know that you are all so well, and, like us, feeling greatly cheered by recent news. The North Africa show really was grand and we out here are all very envious and yet we all know the real thing has not yet started.

'Someday soon, with startling suddenness, the world will know that the show is on. Continental ports and cities will rise into the air in clouds of dust, huge fleets will carry a million allied troops onto enemy territory – many will die, many will live to tell a glorious story to their grand children and we, out here, will feel that life at home will become more free from care, and we will be in a good mood to start a little show of our own to finish the job, as Churchill would say, and maybe then we shall have more to remember than a few million mosquitoes and the Indian monsoon, and maybe then we shall feel that we too have played our part.'

Low morale was a problem only too well recognised by the Commanders.

'Rumours were assiduously spread picturing the Japanese as super bogey-men of the jungle, harping on their savagery, their superior equipment and training, the hardships our men suffered, the lack of everything, the faults in our leadership and the general hopelessness of expecting ever to defeat the enemy. Such stories were brought even by drafts from England. It was an insidious gangrene that could easily spread. Whether morale went up or down, and with it hope of victory, was an issue that swayed in the balance.

The British soldier, especially, suffered from what he felt was the lack of appreciation by his own people and at times of their forgetfulness of his very existence. The men were calling themselves a 'Forgotten Army' long before some newspaper correspondent seized on the phrase.'

[Slim.Cassell.1956.P181]

Tom goes on to say, 'when we have won', that he would save money by travelling home by sea rather than air.

'An extra 2 or 3 weeks will seem but a day when we know that all is over, and that I am coming home, and it will be nice to sail to Cape-Town or to Canada with you and Jan. Maybe you will have some ideas of your own about spending a little money – you may want to buy a house or maybe even a new pram or something. I can never know until I see you again; but, no matter when that may be, I shall still love you darling.'

His war was to last another two and a half years, there was to be no money available for holidays to foreign lands and it has taken 60 years for his 'glorious story' to be told for his grand children and great-grandchildren.

On the 18th, Vera writes,

'It was grand to get a letter last week telling of your thoughts of us. You never seem very far away darling. I always feel you are around. One day, I suppose we shall wake up from this queer, unreal sort of life and find ourselves together again with a grown-up daughter to laugh and play with. Won't she be thrilled to have a Daddy all of her own. She'll look at you with her blue eyes and weigh you up and then she'll bring out all her playthings to show you. She'll expect you to put her dolls in the pram, to have a tea-party with her and to show her pictures and to read to her. She'll be very interested in you darling and she'll come and sit on your knee. Ashy I want you back in reality so much, but I know it's far more lonesome for you without families and without our Janet. We are living for the day you come back.

'I have to be very careful what I say these days because Jan repeats everything after me. I heard her say 'Oh Blimey' the other day. Tonight she had been out of the room for quite a *long time. When she came back in I said 'Where have you been?' and she looked at me and said 'Been to the Pictures Mummy'. I wish you could see her with our little, black kitten. She is fond of it but she simply can't pick it up. I don't think she likes the feel of it. She will wrap it up in her pram-cover and carry it – but even then very gingerly, but she almost shivers when she feels its fur.*

'Jan certainly has a will of her own. We had another scene tonight at bedtime. However, I dealt with it quite effectively by shutting her in the front room all by herself. She kicked and screamed for a while but she was quite ready to come upstairs when I let her out. I do hope I'm bringing her up in the way she should go Ashy but it's certainly difficult at times. You can imagine how she gets a bit spoilt with fond Grandparents around always ready to find excuses for tantrums and always in the background with sweets. I don't think she's really too bad!'

Janet with pram

She presages difficulties that many parents experienced 'when Daddy came home', mentioning the child of a friend.

'I can't forget how disillusioned Graham was about Tommy when he came home from Canada, you remember, the awful child who tipped the milk out of the jug? So disillusioned was he, that by trying to subdue him he frightened the life out of the child. Poor kid – I felt so sorry for him because he was scared stiff of his Daddy, although he certainly was a little monkey.'

They were both worrying over where they would live and what job Tom would do when the war was over. 'I often wonder what you will do after the war Ashy. You may say you will go back to the farm but you know you don't mean that seriously. Have you decided what you will do? It's certainly rather difficult because they seem to have firm ideas about State controlling medicine. If they do, I suppose things will be very different.'

Vera spent July travelling around with Janet to see various relatives and friends. She wrote to Tom with news and she is concerned that Tom is annoyed with her because she had sent a letter which may have offended him. This 'offending letter' is not to be found. On the 29th May she writes all about Tom's family and the farm.

Mail is much delayed but by the 1st August Vera has received an Aerogram from Tom and she is totally reassured that he understands her feelings.

'I received a glorious AG from you, telling me that though you had received the 'browned off' letter I wrote to you, that you understood how I felt and that you still love me. I should have known you would understand, as you always have done, just how I feel, and I adore you for it Ashy. But I was so afraid that you wouldn't understand because you are so far away and would think that I was being very childish.'

A letter of Tom's in July simply says that he hasn't written a letter to her for ages because work has been so hectic. He goes on to say,

'The news from Sicily is really marvellous – we are all greatly heartened out here to see things moving so quickly in the West, and the news from the Pacific, though relatively slow and small is, nevertheless, good. You will of course get little news from this part of the world and I can not say much to enlighten you.

'One cannot expect to hear that the army out here is emulating the famous 8th Army as the conditions are all so different. Nothing can be on a really big scale, apart from the fight against climate and endemic malaria. Such a fight is slow and undramatic, but it calls for hard work and enthusiasm, and it is fairly satisfying to know that we are helping in this and that conditions are gradually improving.

'Glad to say I'm keeping very fit. In this part of India the heat is far less intense than the places I described last summer and the hills and green fields are also much more to my liking than the parched plains I saw when journeying through Central India.'

On the 5th August,

'The Major was posted from this unit and I, as Senior Captain, have been appointed to act as major for the time being. I have been recommended for promotion to Major, but whether I shall get it or not I cannot say. Still, it is a step in the right direction and I feel rather like a peacock walking around with crowns on my shoulders. I knew some time ago that I might be given the job but it was not until today that I was authorised to put the crowns up.

'I have again grown a moustache, much better than any previous efforts. I will keep it until I go on leave and have a photograph taken for you. Incidentally, I want another photograph of you – larger than the last one – of you alone and looking quite serious and your face must be at least three inches in length. You needn't be too serious darling. You may even think of Prestatyn. It mustn't be black and white, but brown [or is it sepia?], and it must be taken by the best photographer available – don't spare expense Ashy.'

By the 16th August, Tom is on leave in Darjeeling.

'It is grand to be able to sleep in a first class hotel, have a hot bath in an enamelled bath, eat really good food, go to the flicks and to decent shops, dance a little, skate a little and just walk around meeting people again. We felt rather lost at first after being away from mixed company for so long. We found it very difficult to make conversation and to refrain from swearing. Still, we are gradually beginning to feel civilised again.

'Tomorrow is the third anniversary of our wedding sweetheart. I shall be with you every minute of the day darling. I am hoping to have my photo taken tomorrow, so I hope it will reach you before Christmas.

'It is over 6000 feet high here so we wear battle dress or services dress and still remain comfortable. It is a very pleasant change from the sticky heat of lower parts of India. We live amongst the clouds here and occasionally get a magnificent view of the Himalayas, but today of all days I wish I were back in Prestatyn three years ago.'

Later that week,

'I think you would like Darjeeling, Ashy. It is built in a bay high up in the hills. It faces North-West so we get a marvellous view of the snow-covered Himalayas on a clear day. Unfortunately it is the rainy season, but, when the clouds clear, Kanchenjunga, the second highest peak in the world, is clearly visible and already we have seen it twice in most unusual circumstances.

'The first time we caught a glimpse of this majestic mountain it was past sunset and rapidly growing dark. Suddenly, the clouds broke and, straight in front of us like huge ghosts, we could see two massive snow-covered mountains, still catching the rays of the sun. In a moment, just like ghosts, they vanished. Two days later, as I was shaving, I happened to glance through the window. The sky was filled with white, misty clouds except for an area of brilliant blue sky straight ahead of me and set against the background of blue was a single mountain peak of startling whiteness – it was Kanchenjunga again.'

He returned to his unit after this leave and on the 22nd he posts a formal photograph to Vera.

'I look very serious but I hope that you will like it. I haven't really changed so much since I left home darling – I just happen to be wearing a moustache and trying to look like a Major.'

Tom's letter of 24th August tells Vera all about Darjeeling with its ethnically mixed population; he says,

'Many of them are evacuees from Hong Kong, Shanghai, Calcutta and England or troops on leave from the Eastern Army or from the plains of India. The rest of the population consists of Ghurkhas, Tibetans, Chinese, Bengalis and 'Muselmen' from the Punjab. The main transport is by rickshaws which are pulled about the streets by tough and hardy Tibetans.'

Throughout August, Vera writes long, newsy letters giving a detailed account of Janet's development and how much fun they had together singing songs at the piano and doing 'crazy dances and acrobatics on the floor'. Janet's vocabulary appeared to be precocious, probably because she received the undivided attention of doting adults all day long.

'Your daughter has been a little devil today. Unfortunately it has been very wet and we were unable to go out so she has been worse than usual. She was like a wasp round me all the time I was cooking, asking endless questions. All day she has been reciting nursery rhymes, climbing on the windowsills, jumping off furniture or crashing her doll's pram into the walls.

'How I wish Jan and I could be on our own sometimes. How sick I am of parents sometimes. They still think I'm about sixteen and sometimes they make me so mad because it's so difficult trying to make Janet behave when they are around.'

The summer was fruitful.

'We went to Dad's garden one day to pick raspberries. It all looked very good indeed and Dad said; 'If Tommy Ashley had a garden like this, he would be swanking about it!'

Needless to say, I squashed him flat by saying that, anyway, he couldn't grow kidney beans like we did! There has been a lot of fruit so we have bottled it and made jam. There are lots of

plums, apples and tomatoes. We are not starving by any means. Dad's hens keep us supplied with eggs too.'

In September, Tom writes to say that he has sent photographs, parcels and letters. He is concerned about Vera not receiving much mail.

'Am I really so neglectful? You should receive AGs and letters at a rate of two a week according to my diary, despite my laziness. For a time, I really was busy, darling. With the help of only two dozen Indians, I was running a whole hospital, doing all the office work, quartermaster's work and sanitation in addition to treating 350 patients, giving them all medicine three times a day and there were times when I was just not in the mood for writing, although it was during that period that I took you for a walk and we saw the moon shining through the trees and I forgot my hospital and lived again for a few hours.

'Sometimes I really don't know how long it is since I wrote to you because I have been thinking of you so much that I don't realise that I am not actually with you and that I'm not even writing to you. One gets like that out here – time does not seem to matter – one just goes on, listening to the news, looking for the postman and hoping, hoping.'

During September, the tide of war was beginning to turn in favour of the Allies on all fronts. The Germans were retreating on the Eastern Front. The Italians surrendered unconditionally to the allies on the 3rd September. As well as letters, Tom and Vera wrote many aero grams, some of which are quite hard to decipher but often contain their immediate thoughts about breaking news.

Tom writes on the 3rd September 1943,

'Four years ago today, the second Great War started – that means that the war is now four years nearer being over. And today our great 8th Army has again moved forwards. The war in Europe should be over before another summer has passed. The Americans and Aussies are moving North from Australia and the Yanks and the Canadians are moving across the North Pacific. Mountbatten is coming out to this part of the world. The Russians are moving relentlessly on. Berlin is going the way of Hamburg and Cologne.

'Sometimes I can almost smell the roses, darling, and see the snow-covered slopes of dear old Corbar. We will be walking hand in hand round the Pavilion Gardens before we know where we are Ashy.'

In an AG dated the 8th of the same month,

'Isn't the news grand these days? We are all hopeful that Italy will soon crack up and that the lads will soon be in France and Greece – wish we could join them'

And on the 10th,

'I am sitting alone in the Mess tonight, and I am listening to some marvellous music on the wireless. From 10 to 10.30 we had the London Philharmonic orchestra playing lovely Hawaiian tunes on guitars. All the others have gone to bed early as we had a late night last night celebrating the fall of Italy – quite one of the best parties we have had out here'.

Letter No 11/43

Capt. G. F. Ashley RAMC
Officers' Mess,
14 C. C. S.
INDIA. 19.5.43.

Ashy Darling,

I have just finished my lunch & I will just have time to write a short letter before the car comes round for the mail. I am enclosing a snap of myself with some of my local village friends. All the other photographs I have taken recently (3 complete rolls) have been completely spoiled somehow or other. I am very annoyed about this because amongst them were some of the most interesting snaps I have taken — including the ones of local villages dancing on 'Holi' day. There was also a snap of me buying cigarettes at one of the many small shops which are found along the road-side in country places. As I haven't got the snap, I am sending a little sketch instead — You will have to imagine that I am there, & that the old woman is trying to sell me an orange for 2 annas. I offered 2 but no luck!

Letter from
Tom
19th May 1943

On the 19th,

'The news is very heartening these days, both from the West and the East, and, if the Americans are to be believed, it will not be long before the Japs are beaten.'

Tom is always busy in the Hospital, with patients and administration, but once the rainy season had passed in October, he takes part in as many physical activities as he can such as horse-riding, swimming and duck shooting.

'The other morning we set off to go out to a local unit to borrow some horses and go out for a ride. We left camp at 6am and as we swung out of the hospital compound onto the road leading down the hill we saw the most beautiful scene I have viewed for months. We were 500 feet above the valley, a valley which stretches for eight miles and is bounded all round by hills rising 1000 feet, and the whole of the valley was filled with pure white mist. In the increasing light of the early morning we could see the hills rising clearly above what looked like a sea. It was a sight never to be forgotten. We moved on and dropped steeply through it all to the valley road. It was cold and damp, just like an October morning in Manchester.

'We eventually got our horses and went for a grand ride about 4 miles around the hills. The sun broke through the mist, which soon began to rise from the valley floor. We returned for breakfast at 8am all feeling terrifically hungry. I found it rather difficult to sit down – still do as a matter of fact – but honestly Ashy it was really grand. I am hoping it will become a regular practice, so we will probably all come riding home on chargers!'

In November he is able to go swimming, always one of his favourite activities.

'Yesterday, for the first time in months, I went for a swim. The river is not normally sufficiently deep but recently it has been dammed up and now there is a grand pool four to five feet deep. After swimming in the pool for a while, Tim and I decided to go up river and look for birds. We swam very quietly and slowly up-stream; only our heads being out of the water and sometimes having to crawl on our tummies where the water became shallow. The river twists and turns and soon we got out of earshot of the others who were still laughing and swimming about in the pool.

'As we rounded a corner we saw a strange little bird hanging onto a reed – about as big as a chaffinch, black in colour with a scarlet head, yellow breast and a white band around his neck. Later, Tim spotted a kingfisher, so we crept slowly across the river hiding behind reeds and eventually reached a spot only yards from the gaily coloured bird. As we watched he suddenly dived into the water and came up with a fish about as big as my little finger. He'd no sooner regained his perch when a heron took off from the bank almost under our noses and chased him up stream, trying to steal the fish. Fortunately the little kingfisher managed to escape.

'The sun was going down behind the hills so we swam back quickly, had a good rub down and a spot of tea and then went back to camp. We arrived back just in time to see a magnificent sunset.'

He describes this sunset vividly and he goes on to say,

Oakfield farm,
Irlam. Lancs. 29·5·43

Darling Ashy, Come + sit on the lawn with me.
The sun is blazing hot + there is very little breeze.
The birds are singing! occasionally you can hear the
cuckoo. Janet is having her nap, so all is peaceful
darling. We have been here over a week now.
At first I hated it + I was thoroughly disgusted
+ upset as no doubt you gathered from a dreadfully
morbid air-letter card I wrote to you. Forgive
me Ashy. I have worried about it ever since +
wondered what on earth you would think of me
for being so horrid. Usually when I feel miserable
I don't write to you until I feel a bit happier
again because I have the sense to realise that
by the time you have received it + been upset by
my worries, I shall have forgotten all about it.
I was miserable + I missed you terribly + I
felt lonely, but that was no excuse for telling
you about it when you couldn't do anything
about it, except that I wanted to tell someone how I felt + you were the only one

Letter from
Vera
29th May 1943

'If you can imagine all these variations of tone and colour and shape my Ashy you will be able to see me in one of those rare moments when I look at something really beautiful and strange and wish with all my heart that my Ashy were here to see and appreciate it with me'.

Later in the same month, he writes to tell her about 'a little hunting trip'.

'I set out with two friends, out in the misty early morning, to go shooting duck. After much argument, we persuaded three of the locals to take us out in their boats. From the road the hunting ground looks like a meadow of rich grass with occasional channels and pools of water. The boats are long and narrow and made all in one piece from half of a tree trunk. They are propelled by punt poles.

'We moved off in line down one of the channels of water and found that we were passing through a swamp with grass and reeds and wild hyacinths floating on water over most of the 'meadow'. Suddenly the channel widened into a miniature lake with here and there little islands of reeds and snipe, diver birds, kingfishers, heron and many other birds the names of which I do not know. Soon the ducks started flying – not in 10s but in 100s. We had grand fun creeping along in our tiny boat [sitting by now in a pool of water] and trying to get close in before scaring them off the water. I managed to get three duck and two snipe so quite a successful morning.'

The same letter, dated 15th November, gives some insight into how the conditions and the lack of progress in the war in India began to affect Tom.

'You have been so much with me during the last week that I have felt almost that I have been talking to you. I haven't kept a record of letters written for weeks now and I just can't remember whether I have been writing regularly or not. I think I wrote an aerogram to Jan a few days ago, but I can't be absolutely sure that I didn't write it whilst I was asleep in bed. Often I dream that I am telling you all about what I have seen and done, and then about two days later I begin to wonder whether it was just a dream or whether I had actually written it in a letter.'

Vera sometimes complains because she had not heard from him for a while and on the 18th November he responds,

'I received an AG from you today dated 22/10/43. In it you tick me off for not writing to Janet. But you are just too late darling, because I wrote to Jan about ten days ago. I didn't write to her before because it just won't sink into my thick skull that our little daughter can stand up and run about and talk sensibly and listen with understanding to what one says to her.

'It is only since you started telling me of the funny things she says that I begin to realise she might be able to realise that a letter from 'Daddy' to 'Janet' is really a letter from 'me' to 'her'. I wonder what she really thinks of me. Tell her that I say she must not pull the paper off the wall again or I shall be very cross.

'I still love you darling and nothing can ever change the way I love you. I shall always be a little bit crazy and your eyes will always be sparkling. I am trying to keep fit and to keep happy. It is no use worrying. If I were to sit down and worry for a couple of years, I should look about fifty when I come home and my Ashy would be fed up with me – so I keep the door closed on worry, I laugh with anyone at anything, I go climbing trees, I swim occasionally and do a spot of route marching occasionally. I can tell you little about my work Ashy but I can tell you that I am trying to do it well for your sake and for our Janet's.'

Autumn began in Buxton. Vera and Tom often expressed their appreciation of the way Emma and Roger provided a secure home but her letters reveal the frustrations that come from living at close quarters with her loving family while bringing up a lively two and a half year old child. Love for her daughter and longing for a return to the life that she and Tom had shared in the first few months of their life together shine from the letters.

In September, Vera writes,

'I wish I could have been on leave with you darling – wouldn't it have been marvellous if we could have seen and done all the lovely and unusual things together? I would love to see Darjeeling – it sounds delightful. Hotel life must have seemed like paradise after your primitive way of living.

'I'm looking forward to receiving your photograph too Ashy. I hope your crowns stand out well so that I can show off my husband Major Ashley, to everyone. I've got four delightful proofs of photos of Jan and I don't know which one to have enlarged. I hope you will approve of her – but I know you will – you will want to pick her up and hug her hard.'

Tom asks her which she wants to buy first when he comes home – a pram or a house. Her immediate response is to say that they must have a house of their own.

'Where we can do what we like, when and how we like, without having to consider other people.'

On the 9th of the month everyone was *'thrilled about the surrender of Italy. It was on the 6pm news last night and I had just put it on in time. It was a grand surprise. Things begin to look very hopeful don't they darling? Hurry up and settle Japan and come home will you? I can't wait for that glorious day.'*

'I went to Lafayette to get my photo done. Unfortunately the 'brown' colouring isn't done anywhere now because they can't get the materials so you will have to be satisfied with the grey darling.

'Janet was really naughty yesterday at lunch-time. She just refused to eat her dinner, she kept throwing spoons and forks on the floor and was generally naughty so I spanked her and put her to bed with no dinner. So, of course, Mum said, probably quite rightly, that you can't always make a child do things – you must humour them. Needless to say, I was furious and I said that no doubt if I had Janet on my own I should be able to manage her much better. As you can imagine, Ashy, the fat was in the fire then. But I don't care; I want to bring Janet up myself and as I said before it's not easy with doting grand-parents around. However, I shall certainly spank her if she needs spanking. I'm afraid I don't care very much what parents think or say these days.

'Last night you seemed very near to us. Janet looked up and said, when I was drying her after her bath; 'Mummy, where will Daddy sit for tea when he comes home?' Of course, I

saw you at once having tea with us, laughing at Jan and teasing her or telling her to behave. I remembered you and me having tea at George Avenue with Janet kicking on the rug, and then you and I having tea in a little café near the park – we had trifle left over from a wedding party - and then I remembered Janet sitting on my knee and waiting for me to tell her where Daddy would sit when he comes home.'

A few days later the proofs of Vera's photographs arrive and she feels a little unsure about them.

'I can't make up my mind, they are good photos but Mum says I look sad on them. When you have looked at them for a bit you like them quite well.

'Janet put on another lunchtime performance. She has suddenly developed a habit of bringing something to the table to play with at meal-times – usually a little motor car. Today it was a duck. I thought it was time she was taken in hand, so I removed the duck. My word what a performance! She hopped off her stool, flew to the door shouting; 'I want my duck'. She stormed around the room and refused to sit on her stool or eat her dinner. She sobbed and 'carried on' generally. This went on for about a quarter of an hour, Mum, Dad and I eating stolidly throughout the hullabaloo.

'Then suddenly it stopped. She said, 'I'm a good girl now Mummy', and sat on her stool and ate up her dinner like a lamb, with two helpings of damsons and custard. Then she said, 'I'm going to bed now.' She's now in bed and I haven't heard a sound. It's amazing though Ashy, how, after all that temper she could become as calm as you please as if nothing had been happening, whereas I felt like a nervous wreck. What a redheaded temper she has. Just like her father? I don't think so – it must be me she takes after.'

October was a sad month as Emma's younger sister, Kittie, died in Tideswell. Her death was expected as she had been ill for some time with Addison's disease. Vera went through what she described as a 'fed-up phase'.

'Ashy, it has been so depressing here this week. They al seem to delight in talking about death and dying and they seem to revel in being miserable about it. Somehow they don't think of it in the way we did at the MRI. They seem to like things to be fearful and old-fashioned. They make me feel that I'm transported back to the Victorian age, surrounded by stuffed birds and antimacassars.

'You will think you have a truly morbid wife now Ashy but I'm not really. I had a grand holiday and went to London one day with Vera Nash. We went to St. Paul's and it was glorious. We went to the Whispering Gallery and then almost to the top of the Cathedral to see the view.'

Kittie's house went on sale at £800. It was 'old and rather charming with quite a bit of land attached to it.' Roger suggested that he and Tom could buy it together 'because there won't be any houses to be had after the war.' However, Vera decided that she and Tom would not want it and they did not want to live in Tideswell. The house had no bathroom, a 'frightful' kitchen and needed new grates and Tom would only have been able to contribute £200 to the purchase price.

Towards the end of October she writes,

'What ages it seems since I saw you although you seem very near – two Springs, two Summers, two Autumns and one Winter have gone by and now it is almost Winter again – nearly all the leaves have gone and those which are left are lovely shades of rust and orange and all the time, Janet is growing up and you and I go on loving one another as if we had never been away from one another.

The news continues to be good, especially from Russia, so hurry up and get cracking in your part of the world.'

Vera was thoroughly depressed by the oncoming winter, dark evenings and the claustrophobia of a fairly small house with no space or real privacy for anyone. However, by the 10th November she writes cheerfully.

'I have quite got over my fit of depression now darling – amazing how soon I recover isn't it? I have joined the WVS as I told you I would. I'm going to the clothing centre on Tuesday and Thursday and to the Library on Monday and Wednesday and Friday evenings. Today there was a 'Clothing Exercise' – the WVS supplies clothes to evacuees and bombed–out people. I never dreamed I would do such a thing but it was quite good and of course we were revived by cups of tea and buns.'

From the middle of November, Tom and Vera begin to send good wishes and love for Christmas. Some mail seems to arrive in about 20 days but both of them describe periods of time when little or no mail reaches them. Vera heard on the wireless that mail to India was likely to be delayed for some time. She also heard that 'troops in India are to have mistletoe and holly so', she said, 'you should look festive.' Tom was hoping to be able to get some sherry so that he could drink a toast as they had done every Christmas since they first met.

Janet continues to cause amusement.

'Tonight we had a grand time at bath time. I hold her at the top of the bath and she goes splashing down to the bottom, covering the bathroom and me with water, but that's no concern of Janet's. She's very happy Ashy and very noisy. Her latest craze is to be a 'wild animal' which consists of dashing around the room like mad, making the most awful snorts and growls, until everyone roars with laughing.

'I think we should have a good Christmas. We seem to have collected quite an assortment of things for Janet and of course we will have a tree. Janet, I know, will be overcome with excitement and so very thrilled with everything. We haven't made puddings or cakes yet, but intend to do so soon. Dad is fattening up a cockerel for the Christmas dinner so we shall be well-fed as usual.

'Janet says that one day she is going to live in another house with Mummy and Daddy and that she is going to take her dollies and her pram and her books and her crayons and all her clothes and that Grandma and Grandpa will have to come on a puffer train to see her – so you see, Janet has her dreams too Ashy.'

Towards the end of November, Vera is in good spirits and writes to Tom,

'Don't worry about me when I sound fed up darling, I recover again fairly soon and things don't seem so bad. It does relieve my feelings to be able to tell you about it, but you needn't worry. Recently I have felt much happier, probably because I have got more to do. It does make a difference to get out for a little while, away from home and even away from Jan – she appreciates me more when I get back and I have more patience with her.

'It has taken until now for me to be anything like I was before you went away. No matter where I was, or what I did, I was desperately unhappy. Somehow it doesn't hurt so much now. Perhaps it is because I'm not 'run-down' any more. As you know very well, although you don't say so, I have every reason to be very happy. Mum and Dad adore Janet, of course, and I can leave her with them whenever I want to. Please don't worry about me darling.'

Vera regularly went to the Cinema with Joyce, Emma or friends and she describes going up to Manchester to see 'The Yeomen of the Guard' at the Opera House, not getting home to Buxton until after midnight.

'Last week I sold chocolate and cigarettes at the WVS and helped out at the clothing centre on two evenings a week, all of which I find quite enjoyable altogether. I'm as busy and happy as I can be without you darling.'

At the end of the month, Vera receives the photograph that Tom had had taken while he was on leave in Darjeeling. Her response to it is not thoughtful and caused him to write quite an aggrieved reply.

'Last week I received your photograph. At first I didn't like it at all – I suppose it was your awful moustache which made you look so different – but now I like it quite well, although at times I do want to pull faces at you because you look so smug. However, underneath the smugness I can see you are still my Ashy darling and I'm really quite proud of the photograph. Janet is pleased with it. She stands in front of it and says, 'I'm looking at my Daddy. What nice buttons he has got and a nice tie and two eyes and a nose and a mouth.'

'Your Mum has got your photograph too and she said she didn't like it at first. I think it gave us all rather a surprise, although now I'm quite keen on my handsome husband.'

Tom's response shows that he feels hurt and it reveals uncertainties of his own.

'I am glad you received the photograph but sorry to hear you don't like it. I am afraid it is a bit serious but I don't like your expression 'smug'. I had another taken with a big grin on my face but it looked so artificial and stupid that I just daren't send it home, so I told the photographer I didn't want it. I think I'll take your advice and shave off the moustache – it does look rather frightful – but it does help me to feel a little more like a second-in-command.'

He has received the photos of Janet taken for her second birthday and says, 'She does look well and happy but she looks terribly mischievous on two of the photos.' He writes a week later, feeling low because his good friend, Caplan, had been posted elsewhere.

'You must be getting quite annoyed with me, but honestly Ashy I haven't felt much like writing letters this week. Jan's photos made me feel very homesick. How grand it would be

if I could just pop in to see you both every now and again. Thoughts of Christmas are making me miss you more than ever. Maybe next year darling we may be together again.'

Just before Christmas, he writes saying that he had shaved off the moustache but everyone told him he should grow it again immediately. However, he hoped to get another photo taken before doing so. He is still waiting for the photos of Vera, and his parcels from home to arrive.

'Sorry to say no more parcels have arrived so I'm afraid that they must have been lost at sea as we have been told that all parcels posted between mid-September and mid-October were lost.

'I do hope the war in the West will finish soon, as I don't think anything really big will happen out here until Germany is beaten, although the lads out here are all keen to get into a really big action. I wouldn't mind having a look at China myself whilst we are out here.'

On the 29th December Tom writes,

'We had quite a good Christmas here. We managed to lay in a good stock of hooch and also got some Christmas cake, plum puddings, crystallised fruits, sweets, mince meat and nuts sent up from Calcutta. I managed to scrounge a little sherry too darling and I drank two glasses at 6.30pm on Christmas day, one for you and one for me. I am not really short of anything except you and Jan, God knows I miss you enough at times. Tell the boys back home to hurry up and finish off the Jerry so that we can get cracking out here.'

'In 1943 the Army had so far recovered its resilience that promptly after the setback in Arakan the divisional commanders began to rebuild the combat powers of their units – The confidence of the Army rose steadily. Beyond the local recovery, two other factors made for reinvigoration. The first was the setting up of a new Allied Command in South-East Asia; the second was its brisk air and promise of action.'   [Owen.HMSO.1948.P43]

By the end of the year, serious action became imminent in Burma; both the Japanese and Allied Forces were planning attacks.

'General William Slim was preparing to go over to the offensive - the 14th Army, under his inspired leadership, had been transformed from the low state it had reached after the agonising retreat from Burma in 1942.'

[Keegan.1989.P465]

Major Tom Ashley

CHAPTER FIVE

～1944～

Admiral Lord Louis Mountbatten was appointed the Supreme Allied Commander of South East Asia Command in November 1943. He set out to integrate the Anglo-American staff and to ensure co-operation with India Command.

'India was the administrative base, the channel of supply, and the training ground and source of so many valiant soldiers.'

Eight hundred miles of the Bengal and Assam railway were militarised. Military roads were steadily improved and airfields were built. Mountbatten had to broaden contacts with the Chinese forces, safeguard a vital air-route and open the Burma Road as well as holding the frontiers of India at all points. 'Bold decisions had to be made and unorthodox methods applied.'

He determined to
'march, fight and fly through the monsoon' – something that traditionally had never been done – and 'malaria he proposed to enlist as an ally.' Following studies of the unhealthiest regions, particularly the Kabaw Valley, special means were sought to 'overcome malaria, dysentery, scrub typhus and other afflictions which abounded there – and by enforcing a strict anti-malaria discipline, the Command did in fact successfully defy disease.
'A still more vital, if less tangible, force had to be intensified – the fighting spirit of the whole command.'

Mountbatten visited the troops and spoke to them directly, saying

'If the Japs try their old dodge of infiltrating behind you and cutting your line of communication, stay put: we will supply you by air. There will be no more retreat. We are not going to quit fighting when the monsoon comes, like drawing stumps at a cricket match when it rains. If we only fight for six months of the year the war will take twice as long. The Japs don't expect us to fight on; they will be surprised and caught on the wrong foot.

We shall fight in places like the Kabaw Valley. We have got anti-malaria devices and we shall have the finest hospitalisation and air evacuation scheme that the Far East has ever seen. The Japs, who have nothing, will have to fight nature as well as us. Who started this story about the Jap Superman? Millions of them are unintelligent slum dwellers with nothing except an ignorant fanatical idea that their Emperor is God. Intelligent, free men can whip them every time.'

[Owen.1946.HMSO.P44]

Mountbatten further raised morale by giving the troops information about the progress of the campaign.

'On January 10th, 1944, SEAC, the troop's daily newspaper, floated down by parachute on the forward positions. It reported an advance by the British forces into the Arakan in the South. By the New Year 1944, the Japanese had reached the planned limit of their conquests. To consolidate their grip upon these gains, they have now to pay the penalty of conquerors – they could secure their frontier only by advancing beyond it.'

[Owen.1946 HMSO. P47]

The Japanese began to unfold their Grand Design to invade India from Arakan in Burma. This area was,

'A broken coast of jungle covered hills divided by deep river valleys' beside the Bay of Bengal. They planned to split eastern India from the west, cut lines of communication and to advance to Chittagong where they 'expected to incite a general uprising in Bengal against the British.' Known as 'Operation C', this headlong attack followed a 'bold and well-articulated plan.'

In February, the Japanese had made significant inroads on this southern front and they surrounded a main administrative centre called the 'the Admin Box'. They proclaimed their triumph on Japanese radio, saying to the allied troops in the Pacific,

'Why not go home? It's all over in Burma. It really appeared to them that everything was in the bag, and so it was. Unfortunately for Tanahashi [Colonel to the leading task-force], the neck of the bag was still open. He had forgotten the air.'

[Owen.1946. HMSO. P54]

The allied troops held their ground, supplies that had been denied land passage poured in by air,

'and the 8000 personnel trapped in the Admin Box under the guns of the enemy on the surrounding hills, fought on, conscious only of the fact that the hour called for every ounce of courage and endurance that the British and Indian could pull forth.
'Every part of the Box was vulnerable to fire, and a glimmer of light attracted an instant hail of bullets. Wounded men were operated on within 100 yards of the spot where they had fallen. - Regularly as the sun fell over the Range, the enemy donned hoods and yet more hideous face masks and came slithering through the tiger grass, whining weird animal calls to keep in touch with each other. Then the bravest defender had to steel himself at his post. Hearts sank with the sun, and they rose again as it rose. Men who had never seen the inside of a church since their choir days invoked God's mercy and strength. Many scribbled their home addresses on scraps of paper for their comrades to drop a line home – just in case anything should happen.

'Some wounded were flown out by light aircraft over the guns of the enemy, while riflemen held off the infiltrating Japanese infantry. Some hundreds of men were carried safely back to the hospitals of Arakan.'

'Slowly the tables turned. The Japanese themselves became encircled and 'with no transport planes to feed and munition them, they began to suffer the full pains of siege. By the 23rd February, 'the Battle of Arakan was virtually over, and the 14th Army stood triumphant on its first great battlefield.'   [Owen. HMSO. P62]

'This Arakan battle was one of the historic successes of British arms. It was the turning point of the Burma campaign. – British and Indian soldiers had proved themselves, man for man, the masters of the best the Japanese could bring against them. The RAF had driven from the sky superior numbers of the Japanese Air Force. – It was a victory, a victory about which there could be no argument, and its effect, not only on the troops engaged, but on the whole 14th Army, was immense. The legend of Japanese invincibility in the jungle, so long fostered by so many who should have known better, was smashed.'

[Slim. Cassell. 1956. P247]

Tom writes on New Year's Day 1944,

'I wonder what the year will hold for all of us. Surely the war against Germany must end this year – and after Germany what? Will it take us months or even years to beat Japan? And, when they are beaten down too, how long will it be before the world is the same again and we can all settle down to the work and the happiness which we have lost?

'Did you all have a good time at Christmas darling? We certainly had a hectic week out here – mostly parties at which we drank and sang and ate lots of good food.'

And, prophetically - 'I think that I should like to come home at Christmas time and find everybody thoroughly enjoying themselves, although I should prefer to come home earlier if possible.'

It seems that some parcels and mail had been lost at sea before Christmas and Tom was anxious for Vera to send him another copy of her studio photograph. He had, however, received a box of paints and 'a curl of Janet's lovely hair.'

'Tell Jan I shall keep it with me always.'

In a letter dated the 13th January, Tom offers some advice which may not have been that well received.

'Your letters always cheer me up Ashy, except on those rare occasions when you are so fed-up that you write a letter which isn't from Ashy at all. I always find that hard work stops me from being miserable – the harder the work, the more happy I am, although even then there are moments when I feel lonely and miles away from everything that really matters to me.'

In the same letter, for the first time, clues about his location are given. It becomes evident that his unit is stationed in Manipur, not far from the border on the Northern front where serious action was to begin in March 1944.

'You will probably have heard of the 14th Army by now – this is the army to which we belong and before the war is over I think that it will have gained quite a name for itself. Incidentally, I am also allowed to tell you now that I have many times looked across Burma from the eastern hills of Assam and on one occasion I have actually set foot on Burma soil. I went over for a cup of tea a few weeks back.

'Maybe it won't be very long now before I can tell you I have set foot in China or Siam or Malaya or somewhere else beyond the Eastern border of India. I hope not anyway. The sooner we can get really moving, the sooner it will all be over and the sooner I shall be able to return to the side of the two people I love most in the world.'

Tom's letters are becoming more informative about the progress of the war and on the 16th January he says that,

'The big shots out here think that we will lick the Japs in 1945. The situation certainly seems more hopeful than it was when I first came out here and met the remnants of the Army and civilian refugees trickling through to India after their epic march of more than 200 miles through jungle and swamp and over the hill tracks from Burma.

'Some day I will tell you all about that retreat – in many ways it was even more remarkable than Dunkirk because there was no navy to help and there was a mere token force of three or four planes. Now the Jap feels the weight of both British and American bombs and he has to meet the guns and cold steel of keen and well-trained British and Indian troops who frequently make contact and rarely come off second best. Fortunately our policy of waiting is proving well-founded – now the men are supremely confident and the danger is far more for the Jap than for our boys.'

Camera film is hard to get hold of anywhere and he writes that films he bought in Bombay almost two years before, and carried with him through the monsoon, have been spoiled 'through old age and dampness.' It was considered a waste of paper to print them in India but he sends a negative home to see if it could be printed.

'Fortunately it is a happy one, as it shows me reading my mail on a morning when I received two happy air-letters from you.'

A reasonable snap was developed. In the original, probably even Tom would not have noticed the line of washing that hangs beyond the tent and it was not to be seen again until the year 2000 - 56 years later - when Teddy Motler painstakingly enhanced the image.

On the 24th January Tom writes that the weather is just like spring and everything seems peaceful and quiet. It reminds him of days that he and Vera spent together when they first met.

'Then I forget India and I forget the war. I think only of the greenness of England, of the delicate flowers and rippling streams, of an English girl wearing a summer dress, gay with colour, sparkling with happiness and my heart is not sad and I don't believe I am thousands of miles from home and I don't believe we will be any different when I come home.'

At the end of the month Tom writes asking Vera to get him some more professional artists' materials. He sends her a couple of his early efforts, with which he was not at all satisfied. Vera eventually sourced some of the items he had listed at the Army and Navy Stores in London.

'You may hear or read about jungle warfare these days and you may wonder what the jungle is like. In this part of the world nearly all types of vegetation are called 'jungle'. In parts it is quite open, consisting mainly of tall grasses and shrubs; in other parts the trees are very tall and straight, reaching a height of 40 to 50 feet before giving off any branches. It is very pleasant under such trees except when it is raining. In yet other parts tall trees are combined with dense undergrowth with many vine-like intertwining shrubs. Still another variety consists of bamboo trees which are very thickly growing and of lovely green and yellow colours. The trees shown on the painting herewith are supposed to be bamboo.'

'It is raining today, the clouds are hanging low down on the hills and there is no sun to be seen, no birds are singing. I am reminded of the days when I was very young and when such a day drove me indoors to look at pictures of elephants and lions in my ABC, or later to read my 'Pickle Paper' or 'Bubbles' and later still to play with my Meccano and Hornby train. How I wish I could just pop inside 'home' now and lie on the rug in front of the fire in the sitting room, build a bridge, lay out the track under the settee, over the bridge and round the back of the piano; load up the trucks with coal dust and match sticks and set off for London or Timbuktu.'

Vera writes throughout January, telling of 'going to the 'flicks', meeting friends and about Janet's everyday development. Both she and Tom refer with longing to their memories of the time when they first met. At this stage, they both talk about Tom undertaking his Fellowship of the Royal College of Surgeons after the war ends.

'Isn't it good to have a really sensible plan. Let's save and save so that we can have a reasonable amount of money when you come home. I'm sure there is nothing we cannot achieve, loving each other as we do, if we are understanding and reasonable and patient.'

This particular plan did not come to fruition. Neither did other proposals such as settling in South Africa or Canada or even Bangkok, all of which they seriously discuss in their letters.

It dawned upon Vera that her remark about Tom looking 'smug' in his official photograph was likely to have offended him.

'Are you still moustache-less? What a shame it was that we all ticked you off about it. But darling, do grow it again if it gives you more confidence and I was only teasing when I said that you looked 'smug'. I love you very much Ashy and I'm very proud of you, so please don't be hurt, as I fear you were.'

On the 13ᵗʰ February she writes about how grateful she is to be living at home,

'Jan has everything she could possibly need. We have had eggs all winter and bottled fruit and tomatoes which we couldn't possibly have had if we had been on our own. Jan still has Halibut Liver Oil and Orange Juice too of course and she had Virol at times so she really does look well.'

In February Tom describes having 'plenty of work' to do. However,

'There are times when I should be happy for the chance to lie on the sands and listen to the sea breaking against the rocks. I haven't seen the sea since I left Bombay in June 1942.'

'We must teach Jan to swim when she grows up, also to ride horses and drive a car, to speak foreign languages and play the piano. [Maybe she had better learn to cook and sew too.] When she grows up she would have no difficulty in enjoying life.'

Later the same month, he mentions sending 'a copy of our local paper called 'SEAC'. It is very good and keeps us all well-informed of current events'.

This paper was edited by Frank Owen, who subsequently, in 1948, wrote the HMSO publication 'The Campaign in Burma', much quoted in this piece of writing.

Sir William Slim met Owen.

'A hefty-looking second-lieutenant was ushered into my office and introduced as Frank Owen. I had strong views on service newspapers and sat the young man down for ten minutes while I explained to him exactly how his paper should be run and what were the editor's duties. He listened very politely, said he would do his best, saluted and left. It was only after he had gone that I learned he had been one of the youngest and most brilliant editors in Fleet Street and had characteristically thrown up his job to enlist at the beginning of the year. SEAC was the best wartime Service journal I have seen. It – and Owen himself – made no mean contribution to our morale.'

[Slim. Cassell.1956. P190]

Tom mentions that he has obtained more film and that he,

'Hopes to be able to take some snaps in a new country before very long, but I will wait until I can take something really interesting – you know topical background. The news continues to be very good these days – Russians still advancing, Americans shooting out across the Pacific, the 5th and 8th Armies holding their own in Italy and even the 14th Army doing a little bit here and there.'

Letters in February show that Vera continues to do voluntary work and she embarks on a series of lectures. If she wants to receive a WVS badge she must attend all five lectures. She feels that this might show that she has done something towards 'winning the war.'

'But how worthless it seems when some people are doing so much more. I went to another lecture this week on Incendiary Bombs and how to deal with them – there was a film too and it was quite interesting.'

The future development of the medical profession in the United Kingdom was under review and Vera wonders, 'have you received your form to fill in as to whether you agree with the Government's proposals?'

Letters in March show how much the men missed their homes and families.

'Honestly darling, you have no idea how much we men miss the companionship of the women we love. For many days, even weeks, we keep our thoughts under control and live as though life was perfectly natural, and we get on with our job willingly, and are outwardly happy. But, just occasionally, the stupidity of it all makes the clouds appear, dulls ambition and makes even work an effort.

'We anxiously await the opening of the second front in Europe; we anxiously await the tremendous onslaught which one day will be launched against Japan.

'I suppose that you are getting more news of the 14th Army nowadays. The 5th and 7th Divisions certainly did a fine job in the Arakan. You will hear more anon. The boys out here are in good spirit and despite the difficulties of their task, they are tackling it every bit as courageously as the 1st, 5th and 8th Armies are fighting in the Mediterranean, but progress out here will either be very slow or very fast.

'It is interesting to hear the men discussing the war. All expect Germany to be defeated this year. Many think that the Jap will then take another two years, although some say six months only. There is certainly no doubt as to who is going to win. Even if life in India, as a man with responsibilities, may change me a little superficially, may make me hard and perhaps bad-tempered, it cannot change me fundamentally Ashy. When I come home again, you will soon be able to make me the happy, carefree chap I used to be.'

On the 14th March Tom is feeling pretty disillusioned with life in India.

'Sometimes I not only feel fed-up but also sad. Two glorious years of life have already been lost to us; maybe two or even three or four more will be lost. And yet how stupid it would be if we all laid down our arms and said to the Japs and the Germans, 'Come you may be our masters, you may take our lands, our homes, our womenfolk, you may teach our children to be good Japs or good Germans or just kill them all if you wish.' We could never do that – it is impossible for freedom-loving people to be subjugated.'

Towards the end of March, Tom sends Vera a photograph.

'It was taken on the edge of Burma, before the Japs started their funny tricks, by an official photographer who happened to visit the Unit a few weeks ago. Hope you like it! The Colonel was away and I was temporarily in charge so Tim, in fun, pointed the CO's sign at me. I am carrying a stick and look a bit seedy because I'd sprained my ankle rather badly the day before – running down the hill to help put out a jungle fire that was spreading up to our camp - but it is perfectly OK now. About two weeks later we left this spot in rather a hurry.'

Tom as 'Commanding Officer'

Operation Thursday began and there were developments on the northern and central fronts.

'You must find the news from this part of the world very interesting these days – especially the news about some of our troops landing by glider behind the Irrawaddy.'

In early March, 10,000 glider troops had been brought from India and set down across the Mandalay-Myitkinya railway. Vera was indeed aware of progress and she writes,

'It was thrilling to hear on the wireless and to read about the glider landings behind the enemy lines – it sounds so fantastic – like a novel rather than an actual fact.'

Owen's description of Operation Thursday can only be briefly quoted here and needs to be read in full to be appreciated.

'Just after 6pm, 'The gliders 'were cast loose. Bouncing, swaying and straining, the aerial train rushed down the strip in a whirlwind of dust, hauled itself up over the trees and set forth over the 8000 foot mountain barrier for the heart of enemy-held Burma. So began a movement that was, until the invasion of Fortress Europe, the greatest airborne adventure of the war.'

Many triumphs and disasters happened that night.

'But there were grim scenes too, where the surgeons amputated by the light of the moon, and there were gliders that crashed far beyond in the jungle with a frightful cry – and then silence fell while men hunted frantically in the darkness for their dying comrades.'
The raid in the South was daring and one which was to have great significance for the progress of the war. Brigadier Orde C. Wingate was a brilliant and eccentric man who, by using audacious tactics, dared to insert his troops 'into the guts of the enemy'.

'It was Wingate's last, as it was his finest, exploit. Tragedy set a seal upon his triumph. Flying towards India the next evening, his plane was lost in a storm.'
[Owen.HMSO.1944.P68-73]

Vera writes,

'Everyone here has been very much shocked to hear of the death of Wingate. I'm sure everyone in India must be too. I wonder if you ever saw him. According to the news, fighting in Burma is going well just now. You must all feel bucked by it as we do here. Every day we hear news of fighting in Burma and I wonder what you are doing and how near or far away you are from it.

'Did you hear Churchill's speech of last Sunday? He cheered me up immensely when he said that he had reason to hope that the war against Japan might finish earlier than previously thought. Spring is here again and everyone seems to be more hopeful of the war being over soon. We are all well and Jan sends her love and says she would love to come to India in a big ship.'

Mail was regularly delivered at this point, and many air-letters took only two weeks to arrive, so a dialogue develops again between Tom and Vera. In mid-March Tom writes in high spirits,

'It is grand to receive mail from you so regularly darling and to know that you and Jan are keeping well and enjoying each other's company so much. How I wish that I could join you in your walks, how I long to roam over Corbar again or to dance a waltz with you again.

'This war may end so suddenly or it may take many years. How bravely and tenaciously the Germans are fighting, but how aggressive are the Russians! How numerous and cunning are the Japanese but how many ships and planes the Allies are hurling against them! In the fighting which has, and is, taking place on the Indo-Burma border, the Japanese are losing far more dead than are the British and Indian troops fighting shoulder to shoulder. It is possible that Burma will be in our hands again before next Christmas; then supplies will reach China in even greater quantities than at present and once Japan itself is attacked, the war out here is as good as won.

'We still listen eagerly to the wireless and wonder when the second front will start. The war out East seems to be gradually speeding up; the Americans are doing a tremendous amount in the SE Pacific. Believe me the 14th Army is not sitting idle. The men out here are in excellent sprits and health and are bettering the Japs in every engagement.'

They were based 'in the hills and jungles of the Assam/Burma border.' In a brown photo album that Tom had with him in India is a grainy snap of 'the Imphal Road', obviously taken from a moving vehicle.

The battles of Imphal and Kohima took place and both locations were near the Manipur [Central] front.

From the middle of March a series of events led to the battles of Imphal and Kohima and would eventually lead to victory in Burma. The Japanese surrounded allied troops in these two tiny villages in the high hills of Assam but the allies prevented the enemy from breaking through the frontier roads leading directly down into India. Allied troops marched many miles to gather their forces at Imphal to resist the Japanese who had crossed the Chindwin from Burma in strength. During the march,

'The air supply squadrons had sustained them. Mail from home and newspapers were delivered to them every day. On the morrow of their casualties arriving in Imphal, they were flown out to the base hospitals in India. The effect of these arrangements on the morale of the troop was profound.'

Meanwhile, the Japanese 'had closed in upon Imphal and were gazing down from the Somra hills into Assam'. They were also pressing on towards Kohima where there were 1500 wounded already in the hospital. The situation was grave and Mountbatten ordered American air-transport to fly in 'the 5th Indian division from Arakan to the Kohima battle.'

'The British forward troops stubbornly resisted the enemy's advance, making him pay 1000 casualties as his gate money for his entrance to India.' The Japanese did not have sufficient reserves to press home the attack and the allied troops in both Imphal and Kohima held out. 'The Japanese assaults crashed like waves in a storm against the walls of Fortress Imphal but it was the waves that broke.'

'The tasks of the air forces of Eastern air command had been laid down in four words. Strike, to clear the enemy aircraft from the sky; Support our own troops with close bombing, machine-gun and rocket; Supply them in all weathers; Strangle the enemy's supply, by destroying his lines of communication, his transport and his depots. This four-fold duty was fulfilled.'
[Owen. HMSO.1948. P94-96]

The battle for Kohima was viciously fought and it took place in terrible terrain with the Allies and the Japanese at close quarters.

'Water was acutely needed. The ration was a pint a day. For a fortnight the garrison had no respite, and never more than a couple of hours sleep on end. The wounded were piling up and the resources for handling them were cruelly short. – One doctor handled close to 600 casualties during the siege. He amputated with a knife which at the end became rather like a hacksaw.'

On the 18th April, Red Cross vehicles got through, the next day the siege was raised and by the 14th May Kohima Ridge was in British hands. It was not until the 22nd June that 'the jaws of the 14th Army snapped together on the Imphal - Kohima road' and the border at that point became secure.

[Owen. HMSO.1948.P105]

'The fighting that ensued was amongst the most bitter of the war, as the two sides battled it out often at ranges no wider than the tennis court of the district commissioner's abandoned residence which formed part of no-man's land at Kohima ridge. The British were supplied by airlift – The Japanese were not supplied at all; diseased and emaciated, they persisted in their attacks even after the coming of the monsoon. On the 22nd June the Japanese troops retreated - and they 'struggled off down roads liquefied by the tropical rains to cross the river Chindwin and return to the Burmese plains.'

[Keegan.Pimlico.1989.P465]

Many casualties from these engagements must have been cared for, and moved on for further treatment, through Tom's Casualty Clearing Station 'up in the hills and jungles of the Assam/Burma border'.

On the 21st June 1944, he writes,

'The Jap is receiving many nasty knocks these days and must be feeling pretty sorry for himself. Our little show is still going well although the Jap still shows plenty of fight. In attack he is fearless and very persistent but the loss of so many thousands killed and wounded and sick will no doubt soon convince him that his attempt to break into India has failed. It seems that each and every Jap is quite prepared to die for his country and our troops, with their Indian Allies, are doing their best to help the men of the Rising Sun to reach their eternal home.'

Vera mentioned to Tom that she occasionally went to dances – usually at the Pavilion Gardens or for American Soldiers at the WVS canteen – and that her Emma did not approve of this. Tom replies,

'I am glad that you occasionally go dancing darling – in fact I wish you would go more often and really enjoy yourself. Somehow it doesn't make me feel the least bit jealous. I love you and know that you love me. I know that it will always be like that. If I think of you sitting alone at home then I feel hurt, but it makes me glad to hear that you go out to enjoy yourself sometimes. [Do you think that I am very conceited Ashy to feel so sure of you? On the other hand, don't you feel the same way about me?]

'No doubt you will be reading quite a lot about 'our' Army these days. Our boys are doing a very fine job out here and before long you will all hear big news. We have got the Japs on toast.'

Vera, Ada, Bessie, Fred and Dot
with Tony, Bill, Janet, Sheila, David and Teddy

Although he mentions 'being busy', Tom says little, on the whole, about what he was actually doing. However, on the 22nd April he mentions,

'I am getting a certain amount of surgical experience these days – sorting out casualties for operation or resuscitation or transfer to more specialised units. Some of our cases go back to hospitals. The 'tummy trouble' I had last week turned out to be a mild dose of bacillary dysentery but I was only laid up a couple of days thanks to a course of sulphaquamadine.'

A letter dated the 29th April tells of the victory of the Chindits, made up of British, American, Ghurkha and African troops, 'beyond the Irrawaddy' in the South at the Battle of Arakan. These successes were due mainly to 'the benefits of our air superiority.'

'I did not tell you before but we saw many of them going over. It was nearly dark when we first heard the planes and we took little notice as planes often pass overhead. But at frequent short intervals throughout most of the night we heard the roar of a giant plane reach a crescendo and then die away to the East and we knew that something big was on, and the next evening we took more notice.

'Just as dark was settling down we saw the beginning of the second air armada, huge planes, towing huge gliders, and our prayers went up to them because we now knew the nature of their journey. – The feeling of remoteness from the war is gone. We are part of a huge scheme. The Jap does not know quite what to do. He failed to defeat the 14th in the Arakan and he will fail to defeat us in Manipur State. – Maybe he will discover that Burma is not a very healthy place for the self-styled Sons of heaven.'

Letters from Vera in April tell of a beautiful spring in Buxton, of baby chicks and games and trips to Manchester.

In May, the liberation of Northern Burma began and Tom's first letter of that month tells of activity.

'Somewhere near the border of Burma. We have had excitement, we have had movement, we have had work and more of each is to follow. Sorry that I have not written for a few days but we have been rather busy. Now, for a few days we are to have a rest although in fact we neither need nor deserve it.'

He goes on to describe his admiration for the tactics of the leaders of the campaign in Burma which was now proceeding on three complex fronts.

'If war were to be fought with toy soldiers I should find it a most fascinating pastime. As it is I cannot help being interested in the various moves and countermoves which we have witnessed in recent months. I can't tell you the full story for obvious reasons but I can tell you that our commanders are showing up very well indeed and things are going very well.'

Since 1942, American engineers had been quietly and persistently building a road, a line of communication from Assam to Northern Burma.

'Under the blazing sun, in dust, in mud and mist, building even by moonlight and paraffin flare, the road makers would advance at the rate of a mile a day. Mountains, malaria and the monsoon were the angry gods who fought the road makers, and water was their master weapon. In 1944, the year of completion, 175 inches of rain fell in Northern Burma.'
[Owen.HMSO.1946.p88]

Despite all the air support that was now in place, 'to reopen an enduring line of communication with China there had to be a Ledo Road.'

By the 12th May, Tom has moved for the 10th time since January.

'We are quite expert at moving camp now. We shall have to work hard to build a hospital big enough to take many malaria patients and we expect to function more as a hospital than as a Casualty Clearing Station. We have had several heavy thunderstorms and things must be getting very uncomfortable for the Japs. You will know from the news that things are going pretty well out here. Our chaps are certainly full of confidence as they are now far more efficient at jungle-fighting than they were two years ago.

'All our thoughts are at home nowadays as we wonder about and wait for the invasion of Europe. It will be a bloody battle, but it will mean a shortening of the war.'

He says how fed-up the men get when they hear news from home about 'strikes and clothing coupons and squabbles about post-war reconstruction.'

'The lads in the Army and Air Force out here are certainly doing their job and it is grand to be able to work for them. One cannot help marvelling at the courage and endurance of the Germans and the Japs and it is such a tragedy that these attributes have been turned to war. But the allies, fortunately, are not only equally courageous and skilful; they also now have sea and air superiority and soon will have land superiority also.

'The second front will hasten the end of Germany and then Japan will either collapse or perpetuate the war with the inevitable loss of the greater part of her young manpower. Out here, Jap losses are much greater that ours. Generally speaking the situation is favourable for us. We in our unit, are in good health and are being well looked after, so don't worry darling.'

In May in Buxton, ordinary events, like Jan's third birthday, are juxtaposed with significant wartime news and Vera writes about both.

'Yesterday we had Jan's third birthday party. I wish you could have been here Ashy. I felt quite sad when I thought of how much you have missed of our Jan. She was very excited about it all. We had a riotous party with three children and six grown-ups. We managed to ice the cake with ordinary sugar and white of egg and lemon juice and she had three candles of course. - She didn't sleep well and I brought her in bed with me. The next time I woke up it was 8am, the sun was shining and Jan was saying, 'Please will you go and get some tea Mummy?' I can't imagine how I shall cope with a husband and a daughter so keen on tea!

'It's been 'Salute the Soldier Week' here and there was a grand procession on Sunday and Jan and I went down to see it. She was thrilled with the bands and noise. The target here is to raise £250,000 – so far they have got £198,000.'

'The Second Front hasn't started yet, as far as we know, but every morning we expect to hear that things are happening. Trains are due to be cut down so I don't know whether we shall get to St Anne's. I also had a letter from the General Nursing Council asking if I would be willing to give my services in an emergency at a hospital near my home.'

Allied plans for the recovery of Europe were under way. On the 4th June, Allied troops entered Rome. On the 6th, the D-day landings began in Normandy and the Allied forces began the long march towards Berlin.

Tom writes on the 7th,

'Yesterday we heard the news for which we have been waiting for so long, and it has left us with mixed feelings – a great feeling of relief that at last something really big has started and at the same time a consciousness of the fact that during the next few months many young men from Britain, America and Canada will soon be fighting to kill or be killed.

'The war out here is difficult because of the country, the poor communications and the cunning of the Japs; we have seen death and sickness, but it is a very small show compared with the colossal struggle in Russia and France. Our thoughts are with our brothers and friends and with those who sit at home and wait.'

On the 16th, Tom writes,

'The news from France continues to be good and if we can really get going there then I don't see how Germany can last more than six months. Nevertheless, the biggest news that we have heard for some time was today's news about the Fortress [bombing] raid on Tokyo. If we can only keep that sort of thing going regularly then the Jap will soon start to think twice about prolonging the war.

'I am still doing a spot of surgery – I have done a number of compound fractures on my own this week and assisted with a few abdominals.'

When he received his Majority it was awarded because of his abilities as an administrator and because of his management of organisation and supply in the Casualty Clearing Centres. For the first time he expresses some doubts,

'I often wish that I had specialised in surgery as soon as I came out here, as I could easily have been graded as a Surgeon and would now be getting excellent experience. Even now, I sometimes think of giving up my Majority and going back to a big hospital for three months surgery and a test to see if I could be trusted with a surgical unit of my own – but losing a Majority means losing a lot of pay and, as it is, I do sometimes manage to do the odd operation.'

Circumstances dictated, or he decided, that he would not go back into surgery at that time and this was to have a significant affect upon his subsequent career.

Ten days later, he writes,

'The situation out here has eased considerably but there is still a lot to be done. Last night we were operating until 2am and I am feeling rather tired this morning, although I managed to get up at 6am to go for a morning ride.'

During early June, the weather was hot and thundery in England and Vera had some excitement at the WVS.

'There was a terrific cloud burst at Glossop, the reservoir burst and the river rose seven feet in a short time. Lots of houses were flooded and many people were homeless and had no clothes so the depot got an SOS for emergency clothing. You never heard such a panic. Of course, they have never had an emergency to deal with before and they simply stood on their heads. However, things sorted themselves out and the clothing was supplied.'

On the 7th, Vera and Jan are on holiday in St Anne's with her sisters-in-law and the cousins, although she had been undecided about whether they should go because the 'long-awaited invasion of Europe' had begun the previous day.

'Although it has been expected for so long, when the news did come, it stunned everyone here. Yesterday, everyone was listening to hourly News bulletins.'
'I was glad to hear that you are doing some riding again; so is your daughter darling – on a little black pony on the sands. I wish you could see her. She says, 'Don't you come with me Mummy.' Of course, a man goes with about three of them and Jan sits there looking very pleased with herself and her hair blowing in the breeze.

'I am surrounded by blue sky, blue sea and yellow sands, by children laughing and building sand castles and grown ups having a well-earned rest. It is very peaceful here and Jan is very happy. Your Mum, Tony, Bill and Bunty came yesterday. Mother had had a letter from Harold so she was feeling much happier. I wish you could see Janet darling. She is running up and down the sand hills and calling to me every time she disappears from view. It would be hard to lose her because I can see a little gingery head bobbing up and down, shining brightly in the sunshine.'

On the 22nd June, Vera sends some more photos to Tom, to replace the ones that went to the bottom of the ocean before Christmas. She is wearing a 'brown morocain dress' with the tiny, ivory elephant on a chain that Tom had sent her. In July, Tom writes,

'We are now settled down again after two months of great activity. The show is not yet over by a long way but our troops have already given the Jap a good beating and it has been a pleasure to work with and for them. Their fighting spirit is magnificent, whether they be Indian, Ghurkhas or British.

'Before the monsoon started, fighting was sufficiently difficult with all the steep hills and jungle for which this part of the world is famous, but in recent weeks, conditions have been much worse. Two or three days rain cause rivers to flood over into the paddy fields and tracks become quagmires and hill slopes are as slippery as glass, mosquitoes and flies abound and the life of the infantry soldier is far from pleasant.

'We, in hospital, are in a much better position. After moving seven times in six weeks, we were ordered to settle down and build a decent hospital. This we set out to do and we were able to select a good site. Now we have a hospital of which we are proud and one of the big shots told us last week that it is the best hospital in the area.'

On the 22nd July, he writes apologising for,

'Not writing for so long but I have been simply rushed off my feet this week – special job – I will tell you about it someday. The news from all quarters is so grand that we all feel that Germany must be out of the war before Christmas and the resignation of Tojo signifies that all is not well in Japan. They are tough little devils but our lads have shown them a thing or two about toughness. Well darling another 40 patients have just come in so I must rush off to duty again.

'We have beaten the Japs out here. Reaction is setting in. We tire easily, we all want leave and soon we will have the opportunity of going – but where shall I go? What shall I do? I want to see the sea, but the sea will make me homesick. I want to climb through the Himalayas and play with snow, but who will accompany me? Soon the five years service out here may be cut to four and home and happiness will be much nearer for us all.'

In July, Vera and Jan go to stay with Fred and Ada at Oakfield Farm and she tells Tom all about their visit.

Vera and Janet at Oakfield

'Janet was reluctant to go to bed because she was having such a good time playing with the dog and doing a tour of the ducks, hens, pigs and cows; it's amazing how very much at home she always seems to be here darling. You would be so thrilled if you could see her, looking very small and sweet and clean in the big bed upstairs.

Janet taking tea
to Grandad

'It is very lovely here just now darling. The rambler is in flower over the archway in front of the door, the other roses are out and the garden is a blaze of colour. Everywhere looks green and lovely.'

Being at Tom's family home made her feel very lonely and nostalgic and she had reservations about her relationships with some members of the family. There were concerns about where Harold might be sent on active service and worries about Eric's health as he had lost large amounts of weight.

Vera writes to thank Tom for the beautiful flowers he sent for their wedding anniversary.

'I can hardly believe that we have been married for four years. It seems an age since that glorious sunny day and the marvellous moonlit night that followed it. Oh darling, I wonder how much longer it will be before we see one another again? Perhaps not so very long now – the war news brings new advances everywhere, everyday and everyone here is very hopeful of the war against Germany being over soon. It hardly seems possible that it will ever end or that one day some people will be together and happy to build a new life once more.'

At the end of July, Tom goes on leave, flying out of Assam in charge of seriously ill patients. He is on his way to Calcutta and Kashmir – many miles away in North Western India. He writes to Fred and Ada,

'Here I am after travelling by air and rail. I was in the air for about three hours, officially in charge of sick and wounded men being evacuated to Calcutta. It was a great thrill especially as we passed over hill-country which had recently seen heavy fighting. Our army is still doing well and has inflicted the biggest defeat in any single battle that the Jap has yet suffered'.

By the 5th August Tom has travelled more that a thousand miles. He is in Rawalpindi, having travelled from Calcutta by road and rail via Lucknow, Amritsar and Lahore. They cannot get through to Kashmir for five days because of heavy rains.

'Rawalpindi is rather a nice town, beautifully set out with wide streets and many fine shops and bungalows. The club is very good too- rather uppish for chaps coming back from forward areas, but nevertheless a welcome change from a tent on the Burma border.'

He eventually reaches Kashmir and stays at a little hill station called Gulmarg, 9000 feet above sea level.

'It is a very pleasant change from the plains around 'Pindi.' We travelled the last 200 miles in a super saloon car from Pindi to Tamarg and from Tamarg we came up here on horseback – a distance of about four miles in which we climbed 2000 feet through magnificent pine forest.

'We entered Gulmarg by cresting a ridge and it was very thrilling to see a picturesque and rambling town covering green hillocks, the hillocks forming a circle around three golf courses and in turn being circled by pine covered mountains rising to a great height – some of them showing snow drifts even at this time of the year. When the sun is shining this really is a dream town – if it were not for the hundreds of local rogues who clamour round and try to swindle you out of every anna you possess!'

He has a good leave but the letters show how sad he becomes when he has time to think about the wasted years that they are spending apart, saying 'The only happiness I have is in my work or when riding a horse.'

Vera writes that the news about the war seems hopeful.

'Even Churchill in his speech yesterday was more encouraging than ever before. The news is wonderful from all the fronts. There doesn't seem much hope of the blackout being lifted here just yet, although they are putting the street lamps in working order once more.'

Vera's letters during August give the usual sort of news about the weather and the harvest and she always longs to bring alive for him the essence of everyday events at home. On the 4th September, Tom seems to have been really unsettled by his time away from the unit and letters written on his return reveal worries and uncertainties. He wants to hear more from Vera than mundane descriptions of daily life in Buxton and from this point a significant change takes place in the tone of their letters.

'Ashy my darling I love to hear of all Jan's antics and all the little things you and she do together, but there are other things I want to hear. The trivialities of everyday life are the things which keep us going and carry us on laughing and talking from one moment to the next; but it is the deeper things of which we think in our moments of loneliness that either make us unhappy or bring a smile to our eyes or a thrill to our minds.

'Of these thoughts we rarely speak to each other. – Inevitably we are turning over in our thoughts memories of the past and worries about the future. Sometimes I feel terribly serious – what shall we do in the future Ashy? And where shall we settle down? Tell me darling, what would you like to do after the war? Shall we stay in England or shall we face a brave new world in a brave new way?'

In reply to this Vera says,

'It would be pretty tough leaving our parents but it would be our own life we were making my darling and Jan would be OK so long as we could take her with us. I wouldn't consider leaving her behind. I am so glad that at last we seem to have started a discussion which will lead us somewhere. I will read books about where we may go and tell you which appeals to me most. Am I forgiven for being an escapist for so long?'

On the 14th September Tom hints at the conditions under which the Allies are fighting and at the ambitious military plans that are afoot.

'Very soon the morale of the Japs will suffer a serious setback. Their leaders realise the fall in store for them – Allied blows fall here and there getting heavier and more frequent as time goes on – their leaders will begin to throw out their men and machines to stem the tide, but it will be like throwing chaff before a storm.

'Churchill says that the Jap will be beaten within a year. – Morally the Jap is *already* beaten, but it will take more than a year to drive him out of the jungles of Burma, Java, and Malaya etc. and to force him from the highways and cities of China and crush him in his home land. – To all these points the soldier in his big boots must plod his weary way, by forced marches through the jungle, fighting the inclement weather and tropical disease, until he can come to grips with their little men [also in big boots] who are holding well-prepared positions and who are not afraid to die. Someday perhaps the world will realise that the invasion of Europe was not the only difficult job to be accomplished in world war two.'

Another letter makes no mention of his concerns and he talks about the war with Germany finishing soon, the possibility of repatriation to England being reduced to four years and even the possibility of Vera going out to India. This is discussed throughout the next few weeks but by the end of October, Vera had heard directly from the War Office that she would not be permitted to travel to India as a civilian.

One of Vera's replies gives a brisk response to his remark that her opinions 'may influence' his decision about whether or not to consider emigration to one of 'the colonies'.

Letters from both of them throughout September show how uncertain they were about the future. Former colleagues at Manchester University advised keeping the idea of Canada 'in the background' because of the danger of massive inflation when the war ended. Tom was advised strongly to consider doing his F.R.C.S. on his return to the UK, but this would mean being resident in hospitals during obligatory senior house jobs. Once the qualification was obtained, 'a salaried post sufficient to live on in a modest way should be obtainable.'

Letters throughout October show that a certain amount of strain was starting to develop between Tom and Vera after so much time apart. A letter from Tom on the 4th reveals the extent of his longing for a return to normal life and it is explicit about the difficulties of two people who love each other so much being separated for such a long time. His openness prompts letters from Vera some of which he may have found disconcerting. Many of the October letters express the heart of their feelings about their separation. Vera recalls how traumatised she was by her parting from Tom when he set off overseas.

'I always feel that a tearful ghost still stands on Stockport Station, and I think that ghost will still stand there until you are safely home again.'

At last Tom receives the Lafayette photos of Vera, and some snaps taken up the Moss.

'You look even lovelier than ever – somehow you look more mature. I am glad you don't look unhappy or bitter. You look a little sad, perhaps a wee bit tired but so steadfast and confident and so very lovely my Ashy. I can hardly write this letter because my eyes keep straying up to your photograph to read there all that I want to know about your thoughts, your dreams and your hopes. I can read only one thing, and it is all that I want to read, that you love and trust me.

'Two snaps I like particularly – the one where you and Jan are sitting in the hay-field and you are frowning slightly, and the other where you are sitting on a fallen tree in our orchard, with your left arm around Jan and your right arm around the little black and white dog.

'Jan means more to me than you realise. She is someone I gave to you as a substitute for myself – so long as I know that she is happy and healthy, so long as I know that you two love one another then I am content. You see I don't know Jan very well darling so I can't talk to you about her very much. No matter how hard I try, I can never create a picture of Jan in my mind. All I can see is an image of you and a miniature image of you. Don't worry about Jan and me darling. We will love each other when we meet.'

At the start of November, Tom is despondent. The Germans have not caved in as had been expected.

Vera, 1944

'I don't think I shall get home in under four years unless the war takes a sudden change for the better. No-one around here expected the Germans to hang on so grimly. News from the Pacific is excellent and the most cheering news we have had since D-Day. With luck out here we should retake Burma in the next few months but nothing can be prophesied except that long and bloody struggles lie ahead.'

Tom is glad that in recent letters he had opened his thoughts to Vera even though this led to some irate exchanges. He disputes the contention that Vera is unable to be independent while living in Buxton and he offers advice.

'When I am confronted with a course of action which is not very pleasant then I try to work out an alternative. If no alternative can be found then I try to convince myself that the course that must be taken is not so bad after all. How you tackle a set of circumstances is entirely a matter for your own judgement and wishes. In that respect you are certainly independent. Neither I nor your father and mother can tell you that 'you must do this or that'.

Throughout Tom's life, this confident view supported him in pragmatic decision-making. It was an approach to problem-solving that Vera always found hard to share, saying

'It is so easy to hand out advice darling – so easy from 8000 miles away. But when I have to live here things don't always seem so reasonable. My emotions get involved too and it's difficult always to be logical.'

Tom enjoyed the lively letters he was now receiving from Vera.

'Sometimes I write provocative letters to you trying to make you talk to me and say what is in your heart. Your recent letters are like breaths of spring and loveliness starting off a new lease of life and hope. Honestly my darling I have felt like a new man in the last few weeks, since you began to talk and reason with me as though we were sitting together by our own fireside.'

In a letter written towards the end of November, he tells Vera that he is due to travel to Rawalpindi again to go on a course and that he is not looking forward to the long journey. However, he looks forward to being able to buy a few luxury foods in Calcutta for Christmas.

'Incidentally we have been living royally for the past few days because we managed to shoot a deer – venison roast, venison Pie, venison curry – it lasted for four days and was a most welcome change from the routine diet. Although we really have no complaints about the food these days as supplies of both tinned and fresh food are really good. Soya is rarely seen nowadays and bully is only served up about twice a week. Pork sausage has replaced the former and meat and veg. rations the latter. Occasionally we get eggs, fresh fish and fresh meat [Australian].'

While he is in Calcutta, Tom buys a present.

'It is very small and I should love to seal it up and send it to you right away but I daren't even risk sending it by registered parcel, so I guess that I will have to wait until I can bring it home myself and then, if you will only say 'Yes', I will slip it onto your left ring finger. I bought a diamond solitaire, gold ring with a white gold setting. I do hope that you will like it sweetheart.'

A few days later he leaves for Rawalpindi and the journey takes three days by train.

'This morning the monotony was relieved by a change of scenery. We began to climb steadily towards the hills; the engine driver came down to chat with us and invited me to ride on the engine. This I did for nearly an hour and from the footplate I watched workmen and stray cows skip nimbly off the railway track as we approached, I learnt how to stoke up and how to work the controls, I watched the glorious panorama of snow-clad mountains unfolding as the sun climbed in the sky and I thought that now I am 2000 miles nearer home, but still so far, so very far away.'

During November and December, Vera writes about the heavy snow that has already fallen in Buxton, and about preparations for Christmas and for Joyce's wedding which is to take place on Boxing Day. Janet has a new white taffeta dress and is very excited.

'*We seem to be hectically busy getting ready for the wedding. Several people are coming from Northampton for Christmas and George [the husband to be] will be here. Don't know where we shall all sleep. I think some of us will be on settees. Wish you could be here sweetheart. We are well supplied with drinks for Christmas and for the wedding. All our friends seem to have rallied round and the result is really amazing.*'

On Christmas Eve, Vera writes to Tom just after midnight.

'*Mum and I have been hectically busy tonight. We made mince pies, cakes, tarts and pies and in between times I made trifles and jellies and put up the holly and mistletoe. The tree looks like a fairy story except for the fact that the lights aren't working properly.*'

'*Your Mum rang and said that Harold would be coming to see us. He arrived looking very fit and reminding me very much of you my darling. If you see him in the near future he will be bringing you all my love and telling you how fit and jolly your daughter is and how well I am and how I am living for the day I shall see you.*'

'*We shall have thousands of people here tomorrow in readiness for the wedding on Tuesday. I don't quite know where we shall put them all.*'

Rather extraordinarily, in the same letter, Vera casually remarks,

'*By the way darling, I had the most pressing invitation to go away for a weekend with a man – all complete with the most convincing reasons why I should go. Needless to say I didn't go, or even consider going.*'

She elaborates on this later in the New Year but it does seem a strange thing to mention in a Christmas letter. The subject of the company of the opposite sex led to some unhappy exchanges between them.

On the 28th Vera writes a detailed letter about the wedding of Joyce and George Blackburn.

'Peace at last after the most hectic week on record. We have got them married and safely packed off to St Annes for their honeymoon – it was a lovely wedding Ashy and a beautiful, sunny, frosty day – Joyce and the bridesmaids looked an absolute picture. We had a crowd here – altogether there were 16 of us on Christmas Day. I'm afraid we have drunk all we had to drink which was quite a lot.'

Joyce and George's Wedding

Tom goes to Calcutta, on his way back to his Unit, to buy Christmas supplies.

'I have been very successful. The list will surprise you – one case of rum, one case of gin, 20 pounds of walnuts, 8 pounds of almonds, 16 pounds of mixed fruit, 12 grapefruit and 16 pounds of dates – I hope they will appreciate my efforts at the unit!'

Just before Christmas he describes how they are 'preparing eagerly to have a happy time - the patients are all very busy making decorations and the recreation rooms look quite festive, red blankets with greetings written in cotton wool, regimental crests made of coloured cloth, locally made Chinese lanterns and streamers and ducks fattening up in the farmyard. Somehow we won't be able to be miserable. We shall all be thinking of the brighter prospects at home and hoping that next year, we too may be home or at least on our way home.'

On Christmas Day he writes, feeling rather tired and depressed with a hang-over from the party held in the unit on the 23rd.

'It was a wonderful party darling. Our parties usually are. In fact our reputation is such that some people came eighty miles to attend. We had a very big tent with a tarpaulin on the floor. Red blankets lined the inside of the walls and formed a warm background for the decorations. There was a bar made by patients and a log fire in the fireplace, a barrel of rum, roast duck and plum pudding and all the food we could eat.'

Despite all this jollity and companionship he finishes his letter still uncertain about what he should aim for in the future, full of concern about the economies they would have to make at home if he were to undertake a fellowship and longing for home and for those he had left behind.

It was not until June 1945 that Tom wrote in any detail about the decisive events of 1944.

'Patrols spread out in every direction slogging through sodden jungle, probing here and there, seeking out every strongpoint and always accompanied by engineers planning new roads and air-fields, building bridges and each and every one wondering, 'How in the name of God can we ever hope to take an army into Burma over this single hazardous line of communication?' But somebody up at the top knew. Maybe it was Wavell or Slim, only History can tell the world about this.

'When the Jap attack started in March 1944 we were in the Kabaw Valley and, as the Japs swept across the Chindwin, penetrated the Kabaw Valley and moved westwards through the hills, we moved back to Palel and there we first learned the meaning of the phrase 'in close contact with the enemy.' Later we moved back still further and settled in Imphal again. Here we stayed throughout the siege, all troops in the area being supported entirely by air. The danger passed and Slim's army began to drive the Japs back into Burma, remorselessly and bitterly exterminating an army whose barbarity was equalled only by their stubborn courage.'

Such were the advances made by the Allied forces in 1944 that victory over the Japanese became certain, although when it would happen was not predictable. By the end of June the battles at Imphal and Kohima were decisively won and the Allies began steadily to press eastwards to repulse the Japanese from Indian soil. In August Myitkyina fell, together with the river port of Mogaung and the allies moved forward into Central Burma.

'One of the prime gains was the clearing of the Japanese from the remaining area which lay between the allied forces and China. Barely two years after the building of the Ledo Road had begun it joined with the Burma Road and became a highway stretching from Assam to Kunming 1040 miles in length.'

'On August 19th 1944 the last organised Japanese Units staggered out of India. - The spine of the Japanese Imperial Army in south East Asia was broken. 'They will never come back' said Slim addressing one of his triumphant divisions. 'In this year we have thrashed the Japanese soldier, man for man, and decisively. Next year we shall smash the Japanese Army'.'
On 3rd December, troops crossed the Chindwin River.

'It was a symbolic and historic occasion. For it had been here, at this very place, that two and a half years earlier Slim had led the British rearguard over the frontier river in retreat. He had led back the largest single army in the world.'

'In December drums rolled and trumpets sang, and the flags of the 14th Army flew proudly over Imphal Plain.'

[Owen.HMSO.1946.P107-113]

Tom's Casualty Clearing Station, together with others, moved a dozen times to mop up and move on the casualties of these battles, to give life-saving treatment and to get the wounded out, where possible, to permanent hospitals.

At the start of 1945 the allies were moving on towards Mandalay. The 'special job' was under way.

CHAPTER SIX
January to May 1945

In January 1945 the Russians captured Warsaw and ten days later Auschwitz was liberated. The full horror of what had happened to the Jewish people, and to other ethnic groups, began to be revealed. In February Dresden was devastatingly bombed and in Budapest the Germans surrendered. By the 2nd May Hitler was dead, by his own hand, and the German Army had surrendered in Berlin. Victory in Europe was declared on the 8th May.

Meanwhile, the allied forces were gathering themselves to go on the offensive in South East Asia and the Pacific.

'On January 27th 1945, the road from India via Burma to China was opened. Next day the first convoy from Ledo to Chunking rolled across the frontier. The land link to China had been rebuilt. - The jungle now lay behind the 14th Army and with it the stealthy and laborious tactics which fighting in that dense darkness dictated. With unexpected speed Slim's soldiers adapted themselves to a war of open country and mobility. - Slim had received orders not only to destroy all enemy forces around Mandalay but to seize Rangoon before the monsoon, which lay only three months ahead.'

The allies were fighting on at least three fronts to achieve their objectives and it was crucial that the 14th Army was supplied by air as it advanced down the central valleys of Burma towards Rangoon.

'South East Asia Command was committed to carry on with existing resources or else abandon its designs. Mountbatten drove ahead. A series of landings and hooks forced the enemy into retreat down the Arakan coast and the 14th Army closed in rapidly towards the great loop of the Irrawaddy. As early as Christmas 1944, Slim had ordered his Corps Commanders to prepare to cross the river.

'By February, rather than make a frontal assault across the river against the Japanese troops who were effectively dug-in on the eastern side, Slim decided to launch a pincer movement. 'The main Japanese Army in Central Burma would thus be caught between the anvil of the 4th Corps and the hammer of the 33rd Corps descending from the north.'

[Owen.HMSO.1946.P118-122]

The Casualty Clearing Station followed the 4th Corps through the subsequent fighting, eventually becoming a temporary hospital, caring for sick and wounded troops as they moved first east towards Meiktila and Mandalay, through Toungoo and then south to their objective - Rangoon.

Vera writes quite cheerfully in the New Year, saying that Joyce and George's wedding went off very well and that she hopes desperately that Tom will be home within the coming year. She also lets him know that Harold was married on 30th December to Marjorie Broadbent.

Harold

'I expect you will be as surprised as I was. As I told you, Harold came to see us last week but he never said a word about getting married, although he did show us Marjorie's photograph. Your mother rang up to tell me the news and she said it was only arranged the night before. I sent them a telegram from us. If you see Harold in the near future you will be able to get first hand information about it all.'

Tom's Aunt Nora, who lived at Glen Holme, 50 Higher Road, in Urmston, charmingly conjured up a picture of the hurried event, which took place at the Congregational Church nearby. She says,

'It came as quite a surprise packet to me. I was cleaning the front steps when your Dad came racing out of someone's car and asked me if he looked all right because he was going to a wedding. I said 'Yes, whose is it?' He said, 'Harold's, will you come, he wants you to be there.' So I chased off those steps – it was nearly three o'clock then and the wedding was at half-past - sent your Dad off with some large chrysanths [white for the Church], put on my better shoes and gloves and was there just in nice time to see Harold and Eric sitting in the choir stalls and your Dad, Mother and Bessie in the front pew. I sat with them through as beautiful a wedding service as anyone could wish to have - how I wish you could have been there and I know your folk were wishing the same thing. Harold and Marjorie were both in uniform. The wedding breakfast was at the Curzon.'

Marjorie

On the 1st of the month, Vera continues her observations about going out dancing, and developing friendships with people, and she follows this up with one written on 7th January.

'Will you help me by telling me your views on a certain question which arose – not really a problem for me because I already knew my answer - but I have thought about it a lot since.

'I met a fellow here who is an alien and hence in the Pioneers. He was very attractive, very friendly, very generous and a ski instructor. He has now been posted. He was good fun – nothing more as far as I was concerned because no man interests me much these days. My life is full with loving you and loving Jan. But his ideas were very different. He thought that I was very beautiful [!] and his one idea seemed to be to take me away for the weekend – which was absolutely ridiculous, of course.'

Vera's view, that her love for her husband and her child prevented her from even considering the idea, was strongly contested by 'the Pioneer' who thought

'I was a modern young woman not a Victorian child, that I was buried in Buxton and didn't know what life was really like and that it wasn't a question of morals or love but a question of living for the moment.'

She asks Tom for his views, saying,

'For me it would be quite impossible – not because I'm lacking in feelings, or because I consider it would be morally wrong, but because I love you more than anything else in the world. I have learnt quite a lot about life just lately and I'm beginning to realise what an innocent I am and I realise too how great an influence a mother can have, for either good or bad, over her daughter. The incident is closed for good now darling, so you need have no fears that I might change my views or my mind.'

From the beginning of the year Vera complains about the lack of detailed letters from Tom. Despite clues in his letters, it seems that she may have underestimated the magnitude of the massive push of the Burma Campaign in its final stages. Some of her letters would hardly have raised the spirits of a man under severe pressure, containing remarks such as

'Don't you want to write to me these days or are you still celebrating New Year?' and [relating to some friends who were planning to have another baby] *'I am green with envy – there are still some people who can plan their families confidently and securely. It makes me realise how much we are missing darling and I wish so much that we had two children.' 'I saw Eric for a few minutes and he looks dreadfully ill darling. I can't get his face out of my mind.'*

On Vera's birthday, the 3rd January, Tom writes very hurriedly to wish her well.

'I am afraid that I have not written to you for about a week. It is good to be back in Burma and on the job again; we are all much happier when we have a job to do. – Darling, I have been called away from this letter four times already and I must close now and get on with the job as it is post time.'

In his next letter,

'The next year should see great changes in the war situation, both in Germany and out here. Things are going pretty well out here as no doubt you know from the papers. I often wonder just how full the hospitals are at home and just how busy members of staff are. There is certainly plenty of work for them out here.'

On the 14ᵗʰ Tom received Vera's New Year letter in which she talked about going out to dances and he responds by saying that he understands about the need for each of them to find companionship while they are apart.

'All I ask is that you remember that your heart is entirely mine and must always remain so. I have had similar thoughts. I have never enjoyed leave out here simply because I have had no companionship.'

Rather riskily, he follows this up by saying,

'Someday, just for the fun of it, I may take a companion with me. It would be just an episode, to be quickly forgotten, but the likelihood of this happening is pretty remote as it would be difficult to find the right kind of understanding companion. I'll bet all this makes you feel as mad as a hatter, but it just shows how much I love and trust you and how much love and trust I expect from you.'

It is likely that he was teasing her, but in the fraught context in which they both found themselves, it was probably not a good idea. He finishes the letter with,

'Write often darling, I am still very busy and actually enjoying this job immensely. I have a lot of news for you, but can't tell you just yet. I am just flying off to look at our new hospital before returning to clear things up here. The Jap won't be in Burma much longer at this rate. All my love, always, darling from the man who is yours.'

A few days later, on the 19ᵗʰ, there are more clues about the fighting that has been taking place.

'Sorry that mail from me has been so scarce recently darling, but we have been working and moving around quite a lot in the last few weeks. I am feeling rather tired and browned off at the moment – I always do after a hectic spell.

'I wonder if Harold will land up out here. If he comes quickly he will find work very hard and very interesting and I think he will rather enjoy it all for a time. This rapid advance into Burma is certainly more thrilling for us all than the static war of the last two years. There will probably be big battles for Mandalay, Rangoon and a few other places, but it shouldn't take us too long to recapture Burma. Keep your fingers crossed for me darling.'

In the same letter, Tom says that he has become Acting Lieutenant Colonel, in charge of his unit, although he is still 'awaiting confirmation from the top.' He writes to his parents

'It has not yet been confirmed by the H.Q. at S.E.A.C but there is a 50:50 chance that I may be allowed to carry on. If I can hold on to this promotion then I should be able to save enough money this year to enable me to carry on my studies in England and have a go at F.R.C.S so keep your fingers crossed for me. I shall probably have grey hairs before the year is out but it is worth trying for.

'Fortunately I have a good unit and we are quite a happy crowd especially when there is a lot of work to do. We are now well inside Burma and we have seen many things indicating Jap occupation and battles. The Japs are falling back rapidly and all the troops are in very good spirits. Food is good, only cigarettes are of poor quality. I'm afraid I shall have to dump a lot of my kit and books as we are not allowed to carry much around these days. Do look after yourselves. I want to find you all hale and hearty when I eventually come home.'

On the 24th January Tom tells Vera that,

'We heard over the wireless today that the Burma Road has been opened again and that the first convoy has already started off. The rest of the war out here is going very well and we expect big battles soon. We do not yet know where we may go from here. I should like to go to China for a while but there's not much chance of us going that way. Burma is a lovely country but so far I have not encountered a climate which can compare with that of Manipur.

'We have had some big shots visiting the hospital recently. Lt/Gen. Sir Alexander Hood from the War Office, Major/Gen.Biggain, Consulting Physician to the British Army, and I have also had the pleasure of shaking hands with Lt/Gen. Slim. He is a great fellow and is very popular throughout the 14th Army.'

Promoted rapidly to a very responsible position, and in a tense environment, Tom had many uncertainties and worries. In his next letter he says,

'When work is hard I can drive myself and my men, responsibility rests lightly on my shoulders and I feel equal to the job, because at such times I know what I want and I know just how to get it, but when things are running smoothly I feel lost, like an adolescent, indefinite, unable to concentrate and worried. I know that our unit is still doing a good job of work. Slim was apparently impressed by the speed with which we settled down in this new site [our second since Christmas] and with the way we were treating the sick and wounded. It isn't the job that gets me down it is the emptiness inside me.

'At 8am when I go in my office I am a strict and decisive leader of men, on my rounds I am cynical and quite hard, but I hope just, in any criticism I make. The officers and men seem to have confidence in me and to like me. They certainly work well for me and yet sometimes in the evenings I feel so small and incapable I wonder how on earth I ever passed out as a Doctor, how I ever had the nerve to open an abdomen and how lonely I am. You will have a hard job to remind me about myself darling, but I need your love very much.'

He would not have realised, when he met Slim only a few days before, just how much they had in common. He too was constantly struggling with doubts and fears.

'I certainly had my anxieties. One of the greatest was the shortage of equipment. I do not think any modern army has ever attempted the opposed crossing of a great river with so little. – What was lacking in material the men made up for in ingenuity, skill, organisation and determination. The only equipment my army had in full supply was, as ever, brains, hardihood and courage.'

'Doubt and fear slunk in upon me. I was asking so much of them – was it too much? In no other theatre would an army have been launched on such a task with so pitiful an equipment. -- And then I walked once more among my soldiers, and I, who should have inspired them, drew courage from them. Men like these could not fail.'

[Slim.Cassell.1956.P 410-413]

It is not until the 28th January that Tom receives the letter in which Vera tells him about the man asking her to go away for the weekend. His response is measured and seemingly calm but with a note of desperation at the end.

'I am glad you wrote and told me about your 'problem'. I can understand it and I can understand his enthusiasm. Your letter hasn't worried me although I did get a bit hot under the collar - I love you and I trust you. Naturally I'm glad you turned him down although I think I could have forgiven you if you had not.

'After all, people like you and me, who are so full of the capacity for enjoying life and love, cannot help but feel keenly the lack of such enjoyment. I know I do, and I have wondered whether it would make any difference to our love for each other. In all probability it would not, but there is a chance that it might. I will not tell you what you should and shouldn't do. You know what you want from life and whatever you really *do* want darling is your concern not mine.

'The war is moving more quickly towards its end and rumour is strong that even Medical Officers will be repatriated after three years and eight months before the year is out. I think I can hold out that long, but I can't be sure! It would be easy for me – too damned easy - as it would be for your attractive friend my Ashy. Do you still love me sweetheart and does the moon still shine on the snow in Buxton? Hold me tight my darling.'

Vera does not receive these letters until the 8th February when she is away from Buxton nursing her aunt in Runcorn.

In the middle of January, although initially reluctant to go, Vera went to a Masonic Ladies' Night with the Ashley family. Fred was installed as the Worshipful Master and both he and Ada made speeches. Vera danced with family friends and she felt that she,

'Knew everyone because everyone knew you and consequently were very friendly towards me. I waltzed with Dad and really enjoyed it and I danced with Eric and shut my eyes and imagined it was you. I loved every moment of it my darling – if only you had been there it would have been perfect. Mother and Dad were pleased with their evening and they did the honours beautifully.'

By now Eric had been diagnosed as having an over-active thyroid but, although he weighed only seven stone, it was hoped that an operation would be avoided.

Vera's cheerful mood continues as she talks about going to a Concert at the Gardens.

'I used to hate going because it made me feel sad and miserable and made me miss you like blazes. But now I can look forward to seeing you fairly soon! – I quite enjoy going and can sit and dream dreams about you and listen remotely to the music and be quite happy. It was really lovely coming home. There was a full moon and it shone on the snow on the hills, trees, paths and roads turning it all into a sparkling fairy world. It was bitterly cold but it made

me feel alive and very happy – it felt good to be alive, to have a husband to love, and who loves me, although he is so far away, and good to have a lovely daughter tucked up at home dreaming her own dreams.

In the early part of February Tom too is optimistic. He is looking forward to the possibility of meeting up with his younger brother, Harold, who has been posted to India within three days of his marriage to Marjorie.

'I received a telegram from Harold to say that he had arrived safely in India and giving me his address. I'm afraid I won't be able to get away to meet him as we have far too much to do here, but no doubt it won't be long before he joins the famous 14th!'

Tom keeps up the banter about 'companions,' and 'handsome Austrian Counts' but then admits to feeling very jealous and concludes,

'Darling, don't you think it is time we stopped kidding ourselves and teasing each other and just thought only that we love each other and always will. Don't ever forget that I am very much alive my sweet.'

It is not often that Tom describes the condition of the patients but in a letter dated the 2nd February he does.

'Yesterday we had a bit of excitement. Two nursing Burmese mothers were admitted with bomb wounds and later an eight months pregnant woman with gangrene of the abdominal wall. A plasma drip was set up, this started off a rigor and we became a maternity home! Unfortunately the child died this morning and the mother is still very ill.'

During February, Vera also took on a considerable nursing commitment when she spent six weeks away in Runcorn looking after Aunt Pollie who had pneumonia. Recovery from pneumonia depended almost entirely on good nursing in those days and Vera was glad to take on this challenge.

'You have no idea how much I'm enjoying myself sweetheart – or have you? It is grand to feel I am doing something worthwhile. There is no-one here except Uncle and me so I have had to be both day and night nurse because he has to go to work each day. However, I have quite enjoyed myself and feel really pleased because she is so much better.

'I expect you are all excited about the European war news. The Russians are doing so amazingly well. It looks as though Berlin must fall this week. There was news too this morning of a British Naval attack on Sumatra. Letters are still few and far between from you my Ashy. Are you still very busy or don't you feel like writing to me these days?'

On the 8th Vera receives Tom's heartfelt letters in which he doubts his own abilities and expresses his terrible loneliness, and she writes in return,

'Today I have received the first really human letter from you that I have had since Christmas. Mail from you has been so scarce, but I knew you were busy and didn't really mind, but the abruptness and sort of deadness of your letters really worried me. You couldn't even feel enthusiastic about all the mail you were receiving – you merely said 'thanks for all your mail'.

'The last bit of one letter made me really mad – 'will increase allotment shortly' – just as if I was a paid servant. But today I seem to have received the key to the whole puzzle. When the rush and excitement of work is finished there comes the inevitable reaction and you feel tired and depressed. You worry and you have no-one with whom you can relax, to show sympathy and understanding.

'I love you with all my heart and soul – I have never loved, and can never love, anyone else. My love and all it means to you will always be waiting – if that is any comfort to you. What do you want me to say? Do you want me to say 'Ashy darling I love you so much and can't bear to think of you miserable and depressed so please find someone who can give you a little love and understanding until you come home to me again.' Being me, and loving you rather too possessively as I do, I can't say it Ashy. But if it would make you any happier I would try my best to understand.

'Oh darling, how much longer must we go on without each other? If we can go on loving one another when we are so far apart and for so long surely our love will last for ever, not merely until we both die but I'm sure it will live somewhere for all eternity – maybe among the trees on Corbar Hill. You know why you have achieved all that you have so far darling – you know it is because your heart was in your job, as I know it always will be. Look after yourself my darling.'

Vera is in Runcorn, leaving Jan behind with Emma and Roger in Buxton for three weeks.

'I feel lonely and I'm missing Janet and longing to get home and see her again. I want to see her happy little face and laughing eyes. I want to pop her into her bath and see her small white body bouncing about in the water. I want to put her on my knee and dry her and smell the sweet smell of her. I want to brush her hair and see it curl into fascinating gold ringlets around her head. I want to chase her into bed and tuck her up and read her a story while she drinks her milk. I want to see her snuggle into her pillow and lift her face up to be kissed goodnight. I want to feel her arms around my neck and her face against mine and I shall know that at least I have a part of you in my arms sweetheart.'

When Pollie was stronger, Vera went to Buxton to fetch Jan and she writes,

'Sometimes I try to imagine you and Jan together. She has missed so much not knowing you all this time. I wonder what she will think about you. She should be very proud to have a Lt/ Col. for a Daddy. I'm very proud of you darling - you must have done a good job and worked damned hard.

'I never realised before I was away just how much Jan means to me and how much she belongs to you and me. I was quite excited coming home yesterday because I would be seeing her again after over three weeks. How you will feel coming home again to us all after being away for three years I can hardly imagine.

'Mum brought her to the station to meet me. She was very quiet and wouldn't kiss me when she saw me but after a few minutes she started chattering and telling me what she had been doing. It was so satisfying to have Janet again sweetheart – to feel I had someone really belonging to me who loves me a lot just because I'm myself.

'Auntie Pollie is still rather weak so I am taking Jan back to Runcorn for about a fortnight to give Auntie a chance to get stronger. At least I feel I am being helpful and that I have done a worthwhile job at last. I sometimes ask myself what I want from life. Of course the answer, I know only too well, is that I want my husband and daughter and a home of my own where I can use all my energy, both mental and physical.'

On the 15th February Tom wrote the first of a series of three letters revealing how confused, bitter and lonely he feels. He has been away from home and all he holds dear, for almost three years; where they would live and work in the future was in doubt; his own life, and those of his men, is at considerable risk as the allies move forward and the war escalates. It is likely that he has seen terrible sights and dealt with crisis situations [none of which he mentions either in his letters or after the war].

His promotion to Lieutenant Colonel is confirmed. The ways of the Army are complex,

'My rank now is really War-Substantive Captain, Temporary Major, Acting Lieutenant Colonel but you need only put Lt. /Col. on your letters!'

In the same letter he cannot resist making another little 'joke'.

'Unless I get really browned off again, I do not intend to spend another leave in India [unless I meet someone who is just irresistible]. -- We are enjoying another quiet spell and I am rather restless. Soon we shall have more rush work to do and my mind will find peace for a while, but how I long for you my darling.'

He writes about hopes being raised high by,

'The exciting news of the last week – the Russians seem to be taking no chances but every day the end of Germany grows visibly nearer and the latest American success on the Luzon, plus the bombardment of Tokyo, make us all realise that Japan is rapidly losing her grip in the Pacific; not to mention our own little war which is going very nicely, although we are only just coming up against stiff resistance.

'The Burmese are queer people. They do not seem to be particularly interested in the war. I am sure the majority do not care whether we or the Japs are in control, many are friendly and offer us tomatoes and chickens, and others are sullen and uncommunicative. It will be interesting to get to the larger towns. Maybe we won't have long to wait'.

A third of this letter is taken up with remarks about 'Sallie' who Tom had met on leave in Kashmir. She had had several sad experiences and Tom talks sympathetically about these, concluding,

'She may apply for compassionate leave and if she gets it she has promised to come round to see you and Jan. I hope she will'.

The next letter is dated the 21st February. After telling Vera how 'blue' he felt after taking over in command of the unit he explains that this is because most of his friends, such as Caplan, Reg and 'Long' John Strong, his former commanding officer, have been moved to other areas and he has little in common with the remaining officers.

'A few weeks ago the Sisters joined us again – the same crowd who were with us before – Sallie, Elspeth, Frankie and Ripp. I like them all, especially Sallie and Elspeth. I play bridge with Frankie and Ripp. With Sallie and/or Elspeth I sometimes go for walks in the evening and at such times I am happy because we talk the same language, we talk about sunsets, trees, birds, the moon and the stars. I talk about you and Janet. Sallie talks about Jeff and Carter and Elspeth talks about John, and we all talk about each other.

'We recapture a little of the beauty of living, our conversation is free and unashamed. I go to bed feeling light hearted and human, with no bitterness in my heart and a longing to hold someone in my arms. That someone is not Sallie or Elspeth, but you my darling.'

He goes on to say that while he has been away there have only really been five people, out of hundreds, whom he has found really 'worth knowing'.

'They all know me and they all want to know the woman and child for whom I have so great a love.'

The third letter, written on the 27th, reveals the passionate misery that occasionally overcomes him.

'We are pretty slack now and two days ago we all went off for a picnic down by the river. It was grand fun. We had a pleasant bathe then lit a fire and prepared high tea. A group of Burmese watched us interestedly and we gave them some food. They were very happy and joined in the fun. I was really enjoying myself.

'I took a tin of milk, punched two holes in the top, and lined up ten little children with their heads back and their mouths open. They were laughing and jostling and, as I moved along the line pouring milk into their mouths, each in turn saluted. I was laughing too. We were all laughing until suddenly I thought, 'Christ, here am I playing around with ten little Burmese children when I ought to be at home playing with the sweetest child in the world.'

'The others could not understand why I suddenly became moody, why I drove the eight miles back to camp at great speed along a rough and winding jungle road; only you could understand the acuteness of my feelings, only you can understand how gay I can be, how sincerely and happily I can love, how angry I can be, how low my spirits, how earnestly I can fight when up against it.

'You know that no-one will ever replace you in my thoughts, you gave me all that is beautiful in life, you gave me life itself. My mind is so terribly active, much too active; I am more restless than ever in my life before. For me the only meaning in life is the happiness which you and Janet and my future career can give to me. I am still all yours and hope always to be so. I love you so much.'

A letter sent from Vera on the 8th March, after she had received the first letter, shows how concerned she is about the general tone of his letters.

'Having spent a restless night of tossing and turning about and feeling absolutely miserable, I don't feel like writing a very loving letter. Lately your letters have been so disappointing Ashy. Every day I hope for a letter which will fill me with hope and happiness once more and

always I am confronted by a hastily scribbled note which could not have taken more than five minutes to write.

'Yesterday I opened a letter to find a report on the war which is anyway a fortnight old and which I have heard on the wireless at least a dozen times until I know it by heart. The rest of the letter was about someone called Sallie and a discussion of her friends and family. Really darling, can you expect me to be very interested or comforted? Do tell her to come to see us. Maybe I can introduce her to a dashing Austrian count – but you had better warn her because, you know, such men are dangerous.'

She tries to conclude the letter in a loving way but does not entirely succeed.

'Jan wants to know why I haven't 'written a kiss', which makes me feel ashamed of this outburst. But I love you so much my darling. I need your letters to put a light in my eyes and happiness into every day and I do feel you might spare me a little time when you write to me. No doubt you are busy but you must have some free time, though no doubt the handsome Lt/ Col. is much in demand. Why should I care? I have my Jan. I have her love and her sweetness and her happiness. But I do care – so much.'

Then, on the 16th March she receives the other two letters.

'This morning I have been out alone, walking over the Common in glorious sunshine, feeling fresh, clean, cool air on my face and I have been thinking about you and about two letters I received yesterday. The story of the Burmese children made my heart ache for you because I know so well how you must have felt when you thought of Jan; she misses you too darling, she should have your love and interest and discipline as well as mine and you need her sweet loveliness too my darling.

'And I thought of your other letter and I thought how foolish you are despite your experience, how unkind you are despite your essential kindliness and how thoughtless, my Ashy. Surely you know me well enough by now – how possessively I love you – and yet you can tease and hurt me with your stories of Sallies and Elspeths and evening walks. I don't know what effect you expected. I hate your Sallies and your Elspeths and I don't want to be told they are longing to meet me.'

Vera changed into her 'smartest dress and most beautiful stockings' and went out for the evening.

'Glad to leave behind anything that might remind me of you simply because I felt hurt and lost and wanted to be among people. Soon I felt gay and fairly happy but still I felt lonely. Whatever I do I miss you darling. These days I never receive any sympathy or understanding, only dull letters or maybe teasing letters which hurt as badly. So far as I am concerned you are free to do as you wish so long as you love me but I shall always be all yours – that I do know.'

Tom received this letter on the 29th March and he begins his response by saying,

'How glad I am that I can still arouse such strong feelings in the thoughts of the one I love so dearly. I don't really want to hurt you my sweetheart, but I do want you to know just what I am thinking and doing. I have never hidden anything from you and I never will, just because I know that you loved me in 1940 and that you still love me in the same way. It is so marvellous to know that our love for each other has not cooled off despite these long years of separation. I belong to you and to no one else.'

Other letters, written by Vera in March, show how she had had time to think more clearly about Tom's situation.

'I can't say I'm sorry for my angry letter because maybe you will realise how I really felt. I don't want to be teased and hurt by the one person I love just because it amuses him to make me angry. Reading your letter again of course I realise that you only intended to make me realise your loneliness and your need of someone to talk to and I do understand my darling.

'Somehow this spring is full of hope whereas all the springs you have been away until now have filled me with a hopeless sort of longing for you. Coming home from the flicks, a dance or a concert, sometimes under a starlit, moonlight sky with the hills standing up against the skyline – always, when I'm coming up the hill I look up at the sky and listen to the stillness all around me and I think about you my darling and I miss you.'

At the end of March she was startled to receive a parcel of Tom's 'personal effects'.

'It seemed to bring part of you with it darling, particularly your cap – Janet has been dressing up in it.'

There was speculation in the family as to why the things would have been sent and they concluded that it was because he must soon be coming home. It does not appear that they even considered that it was because Tom had to be prepared to move immediately, at any time, through dense jungle and across rivers, and the only things that could be taken with the unit were essential supplies.

Their letters continue to trace the progress of the war during March, the time of most decisive battles in Europe and in Burma. Vera writes,

'Last night on the War Report there were actual recordings of the Rhine crossing and recordings from the gliders going to Germany. I wonder if you have heard them too. Surely it won't be much longer now before the Jerries are finished off and then you will be getting more support for 'your' war. -I expect you are all very thrilled, as we are here, about the crossing of the Rhine. Even Mr Churchill is quite hopeful of a speedy victory now.

'It hardly seems possible that Germany may soon be beaten and if only that were the end; if only we could say and know that now all our husbands and brothers would come home for good and we could all settle down once more. - There are no vacant houses anywhere, of course, and the ones that are for sale are terrific prices – ones built for about £450 now sell at about £900. Having a home of our own seems like a very far away dream at the moment.'

Early in the month, Tom writes,

'Burma is a big place and our boys are tearing it wide open. As they sweat and toil we rest, just waiting. During the day the only work is checking stores, rations and casualty returns or holding Courts of Enquiry into 'illegal absence', 'loss of equipment' and so on. No medicine, no surgery, no apparent progress towards the end of the war, boredom, incipient carelessness, progressive apathy, heat, flies and only the conversation of friends to keep one placid and normal.'

On the 10th March he has been swimming across the Myitta River.

'Twenty two times, a distance of well over a mile; I hope to swim the Irrawaddy some day soon if we camp sufficiently near. One of our divisions is now beating up the Japs in Mandalay and another division took Meiktila a few days ago – we are still west of the Irrawaddy, all casualties being flown back to us. At this rate we shall soon be back in civilisation again – a pity really because we all get a lot of fun out of the country village areas – the swimming and the shooting are particularly pleasant.'

Decisive battles have taken place and more are to follow.

'Meiktila, with Thizi to the east, was the main administrative centre of the Japanese 15th and 33rd Armies.' The area contained all their main bases, supplies and road, rail and air routes, 'like the extended fingers of a hand, whose wrist was Meitkila. Crush that wrist, no blood would flow through the fingers, the whole hand would be paralysed and the Japanese Armies on the arc from the Salween to the Irrawaddy would begin to wither.' –

Slim wanted to cause a diversion from the activity around Mandalay so that he would have the chance 'to repeat our old hammer and anvil tactics: 33rd Corps the hammer from the north against the anvil of 4th Corps at Meiktila – and the Japanese between'

[Slim.Cassell.1956.P393-394]

The 14th Army was divided into corps in order to cross the Irrawaddy River, at different points to create diversions and to cause the Japanese as much trouble as possible. From his letters it's possible to deduce that Tom must have been attached to the 4th Corps and the Casualty Clearing Station would have followed in the wake of the fighting troops initially to the west bank of the Irrawaddy River. He writes on the 15th March,

'Sorry that I have not written for about five days but I have been chasing up and down the country and I have just not been able to settle down. The Irrawaddy is a very long river so I don't think the censor will mind me telling you that as I write this I can look out of my hut and see the river flowing slowly by. It is not quite as clean as it might be but it is quite pleasant for swimming. We have been in twice already.'

A week later he again apologises,

'For being a rotten correspondent but, in addition to work, I have many worries to occupy my mind. Visiting generals pop in with distressing regularity and waste much of the time I should spend in this confounded office. We have not been in the place long and are only just settling down.

'One Gen. said 'Excellent show, you are doing very well indeed after such a short time.' Another said 'You are all to be congratulated – a very fine effort after such a few days.' Others are less encouraging. Thank goodness that our own Brigadier is an absolute gem – that is because he understands the difficulties under which we are working.

'We are confident that we do a good job of work – certain it is that we get little rest. The boys ahead are doing a marvellous job around Meiktila and Mandalay and it should not be long before Burma is completely retaken.'

His letter of the 29th March concludes by bringing together his response to the letter in which Vera expressed her hurt feelings with some explanation of the stress that he and his unit have been experiencing,

'We have had a most hectic time lately – dealing with casualties straight from the bitter fighting in Central Burma. It is tough going for the boys up front, but they are gradually cutting the Jap army to bits and it should not be long before we turn out attention to Rangoon. It will be grand to see the sea again and to swim in salt water.

'Today's news from the Western Front is marvellous – the tremendous advance across the Rhine should have a most demoralising effect upon the Germans. Everybody here seems convinced that repatriation after 3 years and 8 months will be certain from May onwards.

'May – the month of so many joyous memories for you and me darling; May – the month when Germany may collapse, Rangoon may fall and so many changes in the picture of war may occur. May – the month when the most lovely little girl that love ever created will be four years old. May – the month when Ashy will think of Ashy and know that love can never die.'

The crucial town of Meiktila was captured by the 14th Army on the 4th March and Mandalay had been entered and cleared by them by the 21st of the month.

On the 1st April Tom is thinking about Easter at home and he's rather concerned about the frankness of some of his letters to Vera.

'It helps me to talk to you – even though it may be only on paper and even though your answer takes weeks to reach me. Life out here is by no means unbearable, but it is so intense – for weeks we may have to work like slaves, with little or no sleep and then for weeks we may be left sitting idle on the banks of a river – chaffing at the bit and being told to 'wait, your time for work will come again.' At such times we are more or less isolated miles from the fighting and it is at such times that I need and miss you most. It is at such times that I write stupid letters to you and unwittingly make you angry.

'But don't be angry sweetheart. My heart sinks into my boots at the thought that anything I say or do might make you stop loving me, because your love means everything in the world to me and I am going to need you more than ever during the first few years after this war is over. All my love to you both always and entirely – Tom.'

On the 8th April, his 32nd birthday, Tom writes that he has received a 'very sweet letter' from her.

'A letter that shows that you do still love me. – Yes, coming home is going to be great fun. Life is just beginning for us. The perfect happiness of 1940-42 will fade into the dimness of the past compared to the memories which the future will excite. The future – hope, love combined with deeper understanding, a greater fullness of life, a struggle for us but with so many compensations.'

The next day Tom says,

'My birthday passed off very quietly ending with a bit of a party but not a rowdy one as we had very little drink left out of our monthly ration. We are not quite so busy these days as things have quietened down following the big battle for Meiktila.'

'We heard today that Bremen had fallen – I wonder how long the Jerries can hold out. You must all be bewildered by the speed of the Allied advance in Germany. The Japs are beginning to get jittery and will not last long after Germany – so expect me home for Christmas with luck. It would be funny coming home to an English winter after so long in the tropics but I guess I would find a way of keeping warm.

'The Japs out here have more or less 'had it'. Two or three more pitched battles and Burma should be ours.' And, by the 14th April he writes - 'Out here final plans have been made for the re-conquest of Burma and it will not be long before the 14th Army will be in a position to sit back and rest for a while.'

On the 21st April, Tom writes thanking Vera for his birthday parcel,

'From which this time nothing was missing; we are fairly busy and I am expecting a very important visitor in a few minutes. Our troops are advancing rapidly on Rangoon and everything is proceeding to plan.'

Four days later,

'It seems strange to think just how much has happened in the world since I last heard from you. Germany has been cut in two, Berlin has nearly fallen, and nearly a million prisoners have been taken. Our troops out here have moved a hundred miles nearer to Rangoon; thousands of Japs have been killed in Burma, Okinawa and elsewhere. God knows how many children have been born into this world of peace and beauty. I wonder just how big a change will come over the world in the next few days and weeks.

'Work is a little easier nowadays and I am hoping to fly down to see Harold in a day or two. – I believe he is by the sea at a famous spot in Arakan. It will be grand to see the sea again even if Harold should have moved before I get there. I shall try to have a few snaps taken - you know, 'brothers meet in Burma after three years'- and all that. Maybe meeting him will cheer me up a bit.'

The visit to see Harold was literally a flying one and Tom was back in his unit three days later.

'I am safely back after an 800 mile round trip – I thoroughly enjoyed every minute of it. I flew over 200 miles to Cox's Bazaar on the coast of the Arakan and then travelled by road to Chittagong as Harold had changed station.

'It was strange meeting him again after so long. Time seemed as nothing. It was just as though I had been off somewhere for the weekend and had then bumped into Harold on my way home. He does not seem to have changed in the least since I left home. I wonder if he found any change in me. I wonder if I will find any change in everybody at home.

We went down to the sea for a bathe and thoroughly enjoyed it – the first time I've been in the sea since Capetown.'

Tom spent the evening with his brother and stayed overnight before he had to catch the transport back to Cox's Bazaar. He mentions that they had 'a snap' taken together. The next day Tom swam in the sea again before returning to the unit.

'Imagine a level beach of firm sand several miles long, great breakers coming surging in and your husband in his birthday suit charging into the water like a schoolboy having the time of his life.'

During April, Vera writes hopeful and loving letters and she seems to be more aware of Tom's circumstances.

'I'm a thoughtless creature to grumble about your letters to me darling when you are so busy and have so much to contend with. Having been out of touch with army routine for so long I had almost forgotten the existence of 'reports and returns' and the ease with which one can 'drop bricks' and receive raspberries in return. Why should I worry about what sort of letters I receive so long as I know you are alright.'

Vera tells Tom that she is making plans to go on holiday to Prestatyn with Ada, Bess and Dot together with all the young cousins. She is envious that Bess's husband, Laurie, is due back from Germany on leave at the end of April. No-one realised then that there would be no soldier's return for Laurie at the end of the war.

While he is at home on this leave, Ada writes to Tom, saying,

'Laurie looked quite fit and well, possibly a bit quieter and as though his mind wasn't on things around him.'

The prospect of Tom's return by the end of the year started a flurry of speculation about how and when they could first meet.

'Your letters are full of hope that you will be home within the year. Isn't it wonderful? I must see you before anyone else – how can we manage it? Couldn't I meet you somewhere – but it is so difficult to arrange because you may arrive unexpectedly in the middle of the night, so I don't suppose we will be able to make any concrete arrangements.

'You will feel like Rip Van Winkle – except of course that nothing will have changed. Your wife may look older but she looks well and she is fit and gay and happy. You won't know your

daughter because the baby you knew has grown and blossomed into a lovely little girl. Our Mums and Dads are still the same although I expect they will look older to you. Anyway it will be 'home' sweetheart and that is all that matters isn't it?'

'I wonder what life will be like after the war – it is an exciting but rather frightening prospect. I wonder where we shall live and where we shall send Jan to school. Shall we ever make up all the time we have lost darling?'

And a letter of Tom's in mid-April says,

'After I have knocked on the door of 22 Overdale Avenue, I will wonder whose footsteps are coming down the passage, whose hand is turning the knob of the door – it *must* be you. I must meet you, my Ashy, before anyone else. How can we make sure?'

At the end of April, the 14th Army races towards Toungoo, a crucial strategic target and one which had to be taken quickly. The Navy plans amphibious landings on Rangoon, due to take place on the 2nd May, and airfields at Toungoo are essential to provide adequate air cover. The monsoon is due to begin at any time.

'Japanese and British alike were converging on Toungoo in desperate endeavours to forestall one another. We must occupy it before the enemy could concentrate there' – The men were driven hard and they had to maximise all offers of help from local forces, notably the Karen people who 'had remained staunchly loyal to us even in the blackest days of Japanese occupation, and had suffered accordingly.' The Karens rose against their hated enemy setting ambushes, blowing up bridges and destroying foraging parties. Battered also from the air, the Japanese lost the race and 'on the 22nd April, with a final spurt, our armour crashed into Toungoo. – We were now 114 miles from Rangoon with seven days to go to the 2nd May.'
[Slim.Cassel.1956.P499-501]

On May 2nd the seaborne assault upon Rangoon begins and the town falls to the allies after fierce fighting.

In early May Tom says,

'I have been travelling up and down the country again; I went down to have a look at Prome and Shwedaung. The former place was most disappointing. It used to be the third largest city in Burma, but now it is a complete shambles overgrown by jungle with only a few buildings undamaged. I am miles away from there now and this spot is much more pleasant but even here one can smell dead Japs [and see them if one has a wish to].'

The Japanese were not well provisioned and many died from starvation and disease.

'The Japanese they killed were fewer than the dead the Allies found. They passed on the roadside wrecked transport wagons in scores at a time, with skeletons sitting at the wheel. Japanese staff cars rusted there with four or five of these grim passengers apiece, and many more lay on the road with their hands behind their heads as though asleep. Their flesh had been eaten by white ants. When they failed to capture Imphal, and in retreat, they had already written their own sentence of starvation on the road back.'

[Owen.HMSO.1946.P108]

Tom must have seen gruesome sights and he shares some of these in only one letter written on the 7th May.

'Everywhere along the roads are burnt-out Jap vehicles, smashed Jap tanks and guns and many other signs of recent occupation including uncleaned-up brothels with sheaths and empty packets all over the place. Apparently, when the Jap leaves a town he retains his women until the last day but one, then packs them off in soldiers' clothing and beats a hasty retreat after them.

'I was inspecting one such establishment today with a view to making it part of our hospital. Viewing the evidence I said, 'My God this must have been a brothel.' A soldier with typical cockney humour remarked, 'Yes sir, but I am sorry we are not open today!'

'The war is not pleasant for the Japs out here right now. Rangoon may have fallen, but the battle still goes on and Japs are being rounded up and wiped out all over the place – asking for no mercy and getting none. The story of the capture of Rangoon is most interesting but I must not tell you about it until I come home, which, pray God, may be soon.'

At some point during early 1945 Tom was commended for 'distinguished service' and twice mentioned in Despatches. These commendations were eventually published 'by the King's Order' in the London Gazette on 27th September 1945 and 19th September 1946. He was awarded oak leaf emblems to wear with his medals; the War Medal, the 1939 – 1945 Star, the Burma Star and the Defence Medal.

Tom told few anecdotes about this period of time. He said that he once had to cut off the hair of a Sikh officer, because it was over-run with lice, and that the man swore him to secrecy about this because his religious beliefs forbad him ever to have his hair cut. Also that, one night, they were surprised in camp by Japanese soldiers creeping through the jungle. Hearing a noise, Tom came out of his tent with his revolver and shot two of them as they appeared near his tent in the darkness. On another occasion, he had to organise the complete evacuation of the wounded from his casualty clearing station because they were in danger of being encircled by Japanese troops.

On May 2nd, just as the Naval assault began on Rangoon, Germany surrendered in Berlin. On the 8th May, Victory in Europe was declared. Tom writes on the 10th,

'We are not very busy these days. The fighting is sporadic and scattered. Japs are holding out here and there but most are trying to sneak out of Burma. Many do not realise what is happening but the majority know that their little game in Burma is over.

'While we still think of war out here, there is peace at home, it is May time, the country-side is green and fresh, there is gorse and heather on the hills and fresh lettuce for tea, the gardens smell sweetly of roses and it will soon be hay-making time.'

By the 13th May,

'Our Janet is four years old today and I am three years and one month nearer to seeing you both again; only seven or eight months to go now.' Tom has 'set up camp in quite a pleasant place on the banks of the Irrawaddy. It still smells a bit but we are gradually cleaning things up and should be quite happy for a while. It is amazing to see the villagers returning in hundreds from the hills now that the Jap is on the run, bringing with them the most amazing assortment of goods – ladies hair shampoos and clips, tins of paint, Singer sewing machines and equipment for a dental surgery – all in storage for the last three years!'

In Buxton, Vera is cheerful and optimistic. On the 2nd May she writes,

'It's May again and the news is marvellous and everyone is full of hope. Day after day we expect to hear that the war with Germany is over – it can't possibly be long now. All the shop windows are decorated in red, white and blue and this morning Mum has been buying flags. Signs of war are slowly disappearing here in England – no blackout, no dim-out, full street lighting and no sirens. It is rather disappointing in a way that the war has not ended suddenly and dramatically – everyone is just waiting for the inevitable announcement now. We rush to hear every news bulletin and have the wireless on as much as possible in case we miss the announcement.

'The Burma news is very exciting too. Today we heard of the landing south of Rangoon. You must be on top of the world because the news is so good.'

She asks him what she should do about his civilian clothes and whether he can buy some things in India because,

'Clothes are likely to be more difficult than ever next winter. I had a vague idea that some of your shirts were too small before you went overseas – no doubt you have put on weight and breadth since you have been away.'

At this point Vera had no real comprehension of the tribulations faced by the men of the 14th Army as they fought their way south through Burma. It was not until she saw a photograph taken of Tom by Harold that the real state of affairs was revealed to her.

Four days later she writes,

'The end of the European war is expected any day now. There is great excitement and enthusiasm everywhere as the German Armies surrender. We are still glued to the wireless. Rangoon had fallen too – and soon you will be seeing the sea again darling. If only the war with Japan were over too. Celebration seems so pointless when there are still thousands of troops fighting against Japan – when my husband is still in Burma.'

On the 8th May her letter is headed VE-DAY.

'Here at last is the day for which we have waited nearly six years. At last the Jerries have surrendered unconditionally – nobody is wildly excited about it because it has been expected for so long now – but everyone is deeply thankful. Not until I see you home safely can I be wildly excited and happy.

'The houses and streets are gay with flags. There is a huge bonfire ready to be lit at the end of the road and the children are having a Victory Tea tomorrow. Janet is very keen to go – 'in my best dress Mummy and I must have some red, white and blue ribbon for my hair.'

I love you. All my love always – on VE Day and for ever – Vera.'

There was great sadness at Oakfield because, tragically on this very day, Dot's brother, Pilot Officer Norman Simister, was reported missing. Although the family hoped desperately that he might survive, it was eventually found that he had been killed in flying operations which took place over Italy. He was posthumously awarded the Distinguished Flying Medal and buried in France.

Vera's next letter is written on Sunday the 13th May – Janet's fourth birthday.

'I think she has enjoyed every minute of it – I wish you could have been here with us darling. We saved all the cards and parcels for her until today and when I put her to bed she said I should write to Daddy to say thank you for the books and to send him a hug and a kiss. We had a party of course with a cake and four candles and a sumptuous tea with trifle, jelly, peaches and tinned cream.

'I shall have quite a job to live up to the efforts Mum makes to please and entertain Jan. Mum will be sorry I know when Jan doesn't live here any more. She will miss her and Jan will miss her Grandma – to her it's as if she had two Mummies – Mum always patient and calm and understanding – Mummy impatient, loving, understanding, often gay but sometimes sad. But to Mum, Jan is her own daughter, small again, and nothing is too much trouble for her.

'We have been very lucky to be able to stay here while you have been away my Ashy. Sometimes I have been fed-up and miserable, as I would have been anywhere – but more so anywhere else I guess.

'Today has been Thanksgiving Sunday. This afternoon we went to see the procession of the Home Guard. Janet enjoyed herself of course, listening to the bands and looking at the flags – I felt rather weepy. We have just heard Mr Churchill – he is still spurring us on to fresh efforts. All week Buxton has been flood-lit and there have been bonfires and fireworks everywhere and parties and dancing in the streets. I expect that tomorrow we will return to normal, but still we shall have a joyful feeling in our hearts because at least part of the war is over.'

Ada also writes to Tom on VE Day and she says,

'We heard Mountbatten speak tonight for your side. I expect you will be wondering, like us, what has happened to Hitler – is he dead or is he hiding? I believe we shall all be happier to be satisfied on this point. When do you think you will get home Tom, will it be this year? It seems almost too good to be true, son, that we can actually think in terms of months now.

'I believe there was great rejoicing in London and we cannot blame them for celebrating as they certainly have had to take it. What a wonderful thing it will seem to them to be even able to go to bed without expecting the horrible bombs which they have been getting for nearly a year now. We had some over here you know and so can sympathise with them. The fact that it is finished hasn't quite penetrated into our minds. I don't think we shall find any change in the working of things for a long time except that there is no blackout, no sirens and no bombing.

'Of course, until Japan is finished off the same way we shall not think the war is over because for us it just isn't. We are all glad to know you are both well and now, once more, 'Goodnight and God bless and keep you'- as he has done.'

Towards the end of May Vera writes,

'Your war seems to making good progress. The Japs are getting some bombing now. Will they fight to the bitter end do you think or will they surrender when the end is so inevitable?'

Brothers, Tom and Harold, meet

CHAPTER SEVEN
~May to November 1945~

It is doubtful whether the British people fully knew the extent to which the Americans were fire-bombing Japanese towns and cities, inflicting grievous casualties upon the civilian population. Despite their terrible losses, both at home and in Burma, the notion of surrender with honour was culturally not acceptable to the Japanese people.

England has become an oasis of calm. Vera writes on the 22nd May

'I thought about you this afternoon as I leaned against a gate watching Janet picking buttercups in a field – I saw Jan running towards me over the grass with her hands full of buttercups, her eyes dancing, her cheeks brown and her hair shining – and I thought of you my darling and all the beastliness of war which Jan and I have been so lucky to escape. For here in Buxton and at home we have been untouched by war except that it has taken you away from us for so long.

'Your letter about the Jap brothels and Japanese dead made me shudder. It must be good to remember pleasant things darling, after such horrors – it must be good to know you have beautiful things to come home to – there will always be other lovely springs and beautiful summers and snowy frosty winters. You have seen and endured so much and I have only known love and loveliness and if I have been discontented at times it was my own fault and because I missed you and still miss you so much.'

By the 28th of the month she has received some photographs taken when Tom and Harold met.

'Naturally I looked at them before I read your letter and you can imagine I got rather a shock to see how haggard my Ashy looked. I do realise that the lighting is bad but even so darling you do look tired as if you had been working desperately hard and sleeping little. It is certainly time you came home for a rest, a little love and some decent food and milk. – I can't help wondering and worrying about you. I want to see your tiredness vanish and I want to see your eyes happy again.

'You look tense somehow as if you have forgotten how to relax. Life must have been hellish at times – but surely it can't be long before you are home now. I feel so mean to have grumbled at my life here darling when you have had so much to put up with and I have so much to be thankful for. I'm sorry Ashy.

'Life goes on much the same here. – Janet and I still go for walks, we stand and listen to the cuckoo, we pick buttercups and we sit in the sun and we are very happy together. We read stories and Jan sits and listens like a mouse. I try to teach her to write her letters until she gets impatient and scribbles instead, I watch her playing with her dolls and hear her humming to herself and I think I love her more every day if that is possible.

'I wait eagerly for your letters knowing that now it can't be very long before you tell me that you are coming home.'

A few days later she writes,

'You must all be tired and weary and longing to be home now – everyone here feels apathetic too after the excitement of VE day. Everyone is longing for their men to come home and to settle down to making a new life. But things go on in the same old way.

'Of course there is no alternative – food must be even more strictly rationed – clothes and furniture too. But we have all the essential things – cigarettes are not scarce here, although I believe beer is not as plentiful as it might be.'

Vera was wondering when and where to send Janet to school.

'I think an Elementary School would be the most sensible and give her a really good start because all schools are to be State Controlled. However, I am putting off the evil day for the time being.'

A letter of Tom's on the 22nd May echoes Vera's words,

'There are all sorts of rumours floating around out here. Many people think the Jap war will be over in six months. Everything is very changed out here now. A reaction has set in after the fall of Germany and the defeat of the Jap in Burma. There is no enthusiasm. All talk is of repatriation and demobilisation and the shortage of cigarettes and expected reinforcements from Europe. Everyone hopes that Britain and America will send out such a huge Army and Air Force in the next few weeks as to confound the Japs and thoroughly smash all their war potential.'

He is concerned that Vera was horrified by his description,

'Of the few unpleasant scenes we have witnessed out here. Don't think that life out here is all sordid and horrible because that is certainly not true. We have much to be thankful for and frequently we are more conscious of the beauty of the country, the lovely sunsets and the cool early mornings than of war and all it means.

'At the moment I am on my way to Rangoon by road and I have called in at a Medical Unit at Tharrawady for lunch. Everything is slowly being sorted out in Burma and it should not be long before the last Jap is cleared out and the country returns to normal.'

In June, to the dismay of William Slim, the Secretary of State for War arbitrarily announced in Parliament that the dates for repatriation would be brought forward and that men would be sent home without delay after three years and four months service abroad. This threw campaign plans into complete disarray. Tom floats the idea that he may be home at the end of September of even in August.

'Mother and Dad wrote – they seem to be in good spirits but very tired and worried about Eric [who was to have a thyroidectomy]. With Eric off duty they will find work on the farm very difficult. If I get home in time for the harvest we could spend a month up there giving a hand. It would help me to rehabilitate myself at the same time. Warn Jan that it won't be very long before her Daddy comes home.'

Tom in June 1945

Vera writes excitedly,

'Yesterday we heard the grand news that service in the Far East has been reduced – which means you should be home sometime in August. Oh darling, will you really? I can't believe it's possible – that means only just over two months until we see each other again. – How will Janet react to you? I'm longing to see you two together. I want to know something definite. How long will it take you to get here once you start? And, later in the month, 'I'm longing to hear from you telling me when you think you will be home. Since they are taking men and equipment out to India by plane – do you think you might be brought home by plane?'

In June, Vera and Janet are on holiday in Prestatyn with other members of the family. They take with them 'food for a fortnight – including potatoes because they are scarce.' They have a good holiday, and beautiful weather, but by the time it's over Tom and Vera's optimism about early repatriation has been dashed because, with the best will in the world, key personnel simply cannot be sent home from Burma before replacements arrive. Many Japanese still remain at large and the question of Malaya is yet to be addressed.

Holiday snap, Vera and the cousins

They are both very disappointed and a simmering disagreement begins over where and how Tom and Vera will meet when he finally does come home.

In early July Tom is 'on the move again,' travelling to Rangoon, 'bouncing along bad roads in a Jeep for nearly a week'. He writes less frequently than usual and the tone of Vera's letters becomes increasingly frustrated. She and Janet have spent a couple of days at Oakfield on their way back from the holiday. Unfortunately, Ada appears to be taking it for granted that Tom will be going straight to the farm on his return and that much the best thing would be if Vera and Janet were to be staying there waiting for his arrival.

Vera fires off three letters in quick succession to Tom telling him exactly why she thinks this is a bad idea. Quite apart from the fact that she does not wish to be reunited with her husband surrounded by in-laws, she is worried that it will be completely confusing for Jan to meet her Daddy for the first time in relatively strange surroundings.

Tom writes suggesting,

'I think it would be a good idea if you were to stay at Oakfield at the time I am expected home. As soon as I dock I will ring Irlam and ask you to meet me, perhaps in London – you could then tell Jan that you are going off to meet me and we could spend a couple of days together before going up to Oakfield and Buxton. – Darling, I want us to be alone more than anything else in the world but we mustn't be too selfish.'

Vera's reply on the 26th July is very definite.

'I shall not leave Janet up the Moss when I come to meet you. If you want me to meet you it will be here at home I shall leave her and from here that I shall fetch her before I go to the farm with you.'

Two days later, she has relented a little.

'Please forgive me for the last letter I wrote you. I'm sorry darling. I have no excuse to offer except that I have felt upset and restless about these homecoming arrangements which are being thrust upon me. – I am bewildered by suggestions and counter-suggestions until I wonder whose husband is coming home – mine or someone I don't know. – I just felt lately that after all I didn't matter very much, that I was only of secondary importance – maybe it's partly my fault for being over-sensitive.'

There are other worries. Fred and Ada are working desperately hard on the farm. Eric has had his operation, and is making a good recovery, but is still in hospital. A house that Vera had hoped they could rent is no longer available and houses to rent or buy are in very short supply. Vera has saved about £600 and Tom will receive some accumulated pay on his return. Furniture is very expensive – a 'utility' bedroom suite costs about £40. They realise just how careful they will have to be with money if Tom becomes a student again while reading for his fellowship. Tom is disheartened about the uncertainty surrounding demobilisation.

'In all probability I shall be detailed to do another job before repat. And goodness only knows when I will be released. It seems that people at home have time only for general elections and strikes. It is a pity that the dockers and bus drivers cannot be regimented into the army and sent to relieve a few of the lads here. It seems a great pity that we should all fight through six years of bloody war and then elect a government full of good intentions and empty heads.'

Vera responds,

'My heart sank when I read your last letter telling me that you would have to see another job through before repatriation and that it would be Christmas at least before you arrive home. Darling look after yourself where ever you go and whatever you do. I realise now just how little anything else matters besides having you safely home again. – Knowing a little about the dangers you have had to face already, it is not hard to imagine some of the dangers you may still have to face, so do take care.'

In August Tom is still 'busy and bouncing up and down on the road to Rangoon and surrounding area. Being close to Rangoon our rations and cigarette supplies are better.'

He is becoming pessimistic about a future in surgery and on the 5th he writes,

'I often think that my chances of becoming a Surgeon are gone. Some chaps are going back to jobs which have been promised them, and which will lead to F.R.C.S., but so far no such

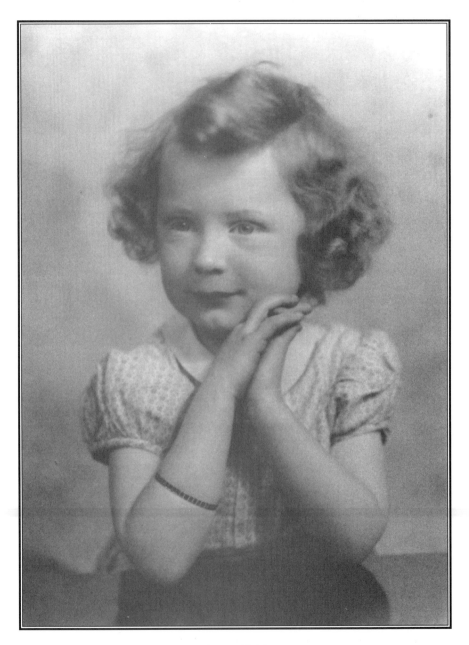

Janet, 1945

offers have come my way.' He talks about other possible career moves and how he would like to travel 'striking out in something entirely new.'

In the same letter he suggests they might buy a 'prefabricated house and get it fixed up in Didsbury – half way between our homes and near to the Infirmary and the Medical School. I think we could afford up to £500 for this.'

Later in the month his pessimism deepens. On the 10th August Tom receives the letters that Vera wrote in July in relation to the organisation of his homecoming. His morale is very low and he is desperately upset that Vera is unhappy and uncertain. He has other concerns too and a lot of bitterness about the situation in Burma.

At this point it was seriously being considered that the regrouped 14th Army would be held in readiness to invade Malaya in September, but later this plan was vetoed by Mountbatten. The Japanese are trying desperately to escape to safety and the last battle of the Burma Campaign is in progress – the Battle of the Break-Out.

Tom writes in despair,

'You are all wasting your time [preparing for me to come home] anyway because it will be months and months before I get home now. Repat is up to three years and eight months again. In this way does Britain honour her pledge to support America in the Pacific, and quite rightly too because we 'old hands' know much more about the job than the bumptious young chaps coming out here now. No doubt, after the monsoon, a new campaign will be launched and the magnificent Indian fighting men, with their British leaders, will strike another smashing blow at the Imperial Japanese Army, ably supported of course by the 14th CCS.

'I have been bitterly unhappy for weeks, just because you are unhappy Ashy. – It seems that war has made us more introspective, more conscious of our own heartaches and less sensitive to the worries of others – even those we love. You can't really talk to people with an interval of 20 days between one letter and the next.'

William Slim is only too well aware of the men's feelings.

'Many of my British soldiers and officers had served continuously for four years in the East, most of them in the often heart-breaking conditions of the Burma front, without, in all that time, a sight of their homes. In danger and discomfort, keyed up under strain, they suffered the soldier's dumb pain of separation. – They heard that men on other fronts got home leave. Their own newspaper SEAC was full of articles and letters urging the return home of men with long service in South East Asia. – The men who had served longest were key. If we sent them home without replacement, neither our British nor our Indian formations could continue to fight efficiently – but among some of them the élan which they had shown for so long, began to fade. To their honour my men endured to the end; never did they shirk duty or hesitate to enter battle, but the strain was telling on them.'

During July, the Japanese continued to fight relentlessly despite the fact that 'Few armies in their situation would have thought of anything but surrender. Yet, when our aircraft showered the areas in which they were with leaflets inviting surrender and promising good treatment, there was no response. Instead, Sakurai collected his men and prepared to break out.'

[Slim.Cassell.1956.P520-524]

Despite their losses and the terrible fire-bombing inflicted by the Americans, the Japanese still will not consider surrender; 'no-one dared speak of peace, and over 400 [Japanese] people who favoured negotiation were arrested.'

'In midsummer the American government began both to lose patience at Japan's intransigence and to yield to the temptation to end the war in a unique, spectacular and incontestably decisive way. – On 26th July the Potsdam Proclamation was broadcast to Japan, threatening the 'utter destruction of the Japanese homeland' unless the imperial government offered its unconditional surrender. Since 16th July President Truman had known that 'utter destruction' lay within the US power, for on that day the first atomic weapon had been successfully detonated.' Churchill was consulted, and Stalin informed; an order was issued to the Strategic Air Force commander to 'deliver its first special bomb as soon as the weather will permit visual bombing after about 3rd August 1945.' The attempt to bring the war 'to an end by the use of a revolutionary super-weapon had been decided.'

On the 6th and 9th August, the atomic bomb was dropped on Hiroshima and Nagasaki. On the 8th, the Russians declared war on Japan, opening an immediate offensive on Manchuria. By the 15th, Emperor Hirohito had surrendered unconditionally'; [but equivocally]

'Explaining that the war has 'turned out not necessarily to Japan's advantage' and that the enemy had begun 'to employ a new and most cruel bomb', he called upon them, in a series of strange and obscure phrases which never mentioned surrender, to accept the coming of peace.'

[Keegan.Pimlico.1997.P482- 488]

It is difficult to say how aware Tom is that the Atomic Bomb has been used when he writes to Vera on the 13th. as he does not mention the use of atomic weapons in his letters at all; however, he knows about the surrender.

'Big news is expected from Tokyo so it looks as though I shall soon be out of a job; and then what? Home – where? Job - what? How strange it is that with the end of the war imminent my worries are increased a hundred fold. – If the cost of living is really so great – with houses, furniture and clothes at such a premium – it looks as though I shall have to give up all ambition and settle down either as a GP or to army doctoring. – I doubt if I could stand four or five years of swotting on a meagre income anyway.

'We thought little of security in those crazy selfish days of 1940 when we reached for, and caught, a star. Luck has been with us so far, more luck than we dared to hope for, and yet we do nothing but grumble. We are tired, we are lonely, our nerves are on edge and we have missed each other for far too long. A little rest, a cup of tea, a walk by the stream in the Dale, a look, a kiss – be patient my darling. I love you.'

On the 10th August Vera writes jubilantly,

'The news this week had been simply stupendous – Atomic bombs, Russia joining in the war against Japan and today, the probable surrender of Japan to the Allies. Were you half

expecting surrender or did you expect, as we did, that the Japs would fight to the bitter end? Even when the news of the atomic bomb broke people were doubtful. There is excitement and anticipation in the air again. - All I really want to tell you is that I love you and I want you safely home again.'

Writing two days later, she says that, although the official surrender has still not taken place,

'People have been celebrating everywhere, including Rangoon, according to the news. I can scarcely believe it can be true – that the world may be at peace again, that eventually everyone in the forces will come home again and start life again with their families and friends; although it will be many years before the world is straightened out once more. It will be a world of grim reality. I wonder what Janet will think about you sweetheart and how you will like having a daughter. I'm glad she is no longer a baby. I think she is much more interesting now that she can talk and understand what you are saying to her – she is a sensible little girl and I think she will soon get used to you.'

They both write about VJ day, remarking that peace came almost exactly on the fifth anniversary of their wedding. Vera is staying with friends in Northampton.

'From the window I can see flags blowing to celebrate the end of the Japanese war and yet on the news we still hear that the Japs are fighting on in Burma and that we are still losing planes to suicide attacks. There have been great celebrations here – street parties with tea for the children and bonfires and roast potatoes and dancing. Look after yourself darling and hurry home.'

Celebrations are low-key in Burma and there is a very demanding job still to be done; this means that Tom will go to Bangkok. He writes on the 21st August,

'With the war over and release speeded up the end of the year may see me out of the army. – Out here remains the job of treating the many thousands of returning prisoners of war. They, of course, will be given priority sailings in ships bound for England, so other chaps due for repat. will have to wait yet a little longer. If shipping is available, Christmas should see most of us home, so here's hoping!'

Vera is full of remorse about upsetting Tom in relation to plans for his return. She resolves to make no more fuss about having a home of their own or where and when she and Tom will meet - which she now says can be at Oakfield.

'Please forgive me darling and don't be unhappy any more. I want to see you so much. Don't let me spoil the happiness we have been looking forward to for so long. I was upset and miserable but only because my love for you drowned all the consideration I should have for other people. Mother has no idea about how I felt about her suggestions, so there is no reason why we should not all be happy at Oakfield.'

A few days later she has received several letters from Tom,

'Some hopeful, some despairing, some sad, some gay; what has happened to us darling? We are both longing to see each other and yet we grumble to each other about first one thing and

then another. Let's wait until you get home before we worry about the problems. I know I started all the silly bickering and I realise it matters very little where I meet you so long as you arrive home safely. So many wives cannot look forward to meeting their husbands again.'

By the end of August Tom's final job in Burma is under way, and,

'Day by day we wait for news of Allied troops landing in Singapore and Siam. Apparently the Japs don't all realise that the war is over, and 'little' battles are still being fought here and there in Burma. The sooner our troops reach Bangkok and Singapore the sooner our 60,000 prisoners will be released.

'Many of them will be sick, very sick, and our job will not be finished until they have been dealt with so you see we still have a job of work to do, although not the job I referred to earlier. A month ago I fully expected to be involved in an amphibian attack on Malaya or Singapore. This, I hope, will not now be necessary.

'Don't forget to get some mistletoe in for Christmas. You know how shy I am.'

Even by the 30th of the month there are conflicting opinions about whether repatriation will take place before or after Christmas. Tom and Harold meet up again briefly.

At the end of a letter written on the 3rd September, Tom says,
'I have got a job to do and I hope to see the cats and the twins tomorrow!'

He is on his way by air to Siam, flying to Bangkok. Despite the declaration of victory against Japan in August, the final, formal surrender of the enemy in South East Asia was delayed. It finally took place on an American ship in Tokyo Bay on the 2nd September 1945,

'The delay could have had most serious consequences for our prisoners in Japanese hands. Men were daily dying in their foul camps; thousands were at their limit of weakness and exhaustion. Many more could have died pathetically at the moment of rescue. The relief teams parachuted into the camps – but could not bring with them great quantities of stores, medicine or clothing – the evacuation of the prisoners to Burma had to await the arrival of our troops.

The state of these camps and their wretched inmates can only be realised by those who saw them at that time. They were little more than barbed wire enclosures in which wild beasts might have been herded together. The gaolers were at the best callously indifferent to suffering, or, at the worst, bestially sadistic. – It was horrifying to see the prisoners moving slowly about these sordid camps – emaciated, walking skeletons, covered in sores and mostly naked but for the ragged shorts they had worn for years.

There can be no excuse for a nation which as a matter of policy treats its prisoners of war in this way, and no honour for an army, however brave, which willingly makes itself the instrument of such inhumanity to the helpless. On the 3rd September, our first detachments, mainly medical units to assist the prisoners, were landed by air from Bangkok.'

[Slim.Cassell.1956.P531]

Tom writes on the 4th of September from Bangkok where he treats prisoners who have already received some medical attention before they left the camps. As usual, he says little about his work; he writes,

'Generally the prisoners are in good shape physically and mentally, but many seem to have difficulty in bringing themselves back to reality and are very vague in their thoughts and speech.' A few days later he writes, 'We are extremely busy out here looking after the returning P.O.W.s and believe me it is a treat to see their happy faces and to notice how rapidly their health improves.'

He goes on to say,

'How strange it is to 'see so many Japs around and to be driven about by tough Jap soldiers in Staff cars and trucks once employed by the Jap Army. The locals seem very friendly and it is a pleasant change to hear cheers as we pass along the streets.'

Throughout September, Vera hears little from Tom because he is so busy, his life is full of activity and he is very fascinated by Bangkok. Her mind is full of worries about where they are going to live and whether they should rent or try to buy a house.

'I went to the Town Hall to enquire about prefabricated houses which are erected in 'colonies' – you know our front door would be about two yards from the next door. I'm sure you wouldn't like them darling. You can't just buy one and put it up where you like. Another alternative would be to take a furnished house, and to pay about £3 a week which is senseless, or we could rent one if we can get one which is doubtful.

'The days and weeks seem to crawl by – the waiting is worse than all the rest of the time you have been away – except of course for the glorious anticipation in the atmosphere, the lovely thought of seeing you again. The canteen has closed now – all the troops have departed – so there is very little social life these days apart from the flicks.'

On the 8th and the 13th September Tom writes glowingly about Bangkok.

'It is a beautiful city and the people are extremely friendly – the children and the men cheering us as we go by and the women smiling and waving. The shops are full of goods but I shall just buy a few mementos as the prices are very high. I certainly am getting a fine chance to see the world and making the most of it too.

'I have already lavishly partaken of the best that Chinese and Siamese kitchens can offer. Can you imagine me dining with rich Chinese traders, eating sharks fin, swallows nests, pigeon eggs, roast sucking pig or eating Siamese curry with prawns and salad and shrimp, roast duck, fresh lettuce and wines from Indo-China.

'For the first time since leaving home I have encountered a city which makes me think I would like us to live there and I am eagerly exploring the possibilities.'

And in his next letter later in September,

'Bangkok is a city of promise and I have almost made a definite plan to come out here. I can rent a house, I have been promised a loan of as much cash as necessary to establish myself, I have made tentative arrangements to work with other doctors on a rota basis and I have made many useful local contacts. – Janet would need a governess; the climate is quite good for most

137

of the year and not unduly hard on Europeans. – I think it is good Ashy and I want to get in now – I know that we could be happy here and, I believe, successful. There is no English doctor here and already several influential people have urged me to stay.'

Vera's reply is weary, she is not impressed and on the 28th she writes,

'I refuse to make any comment on your idea of settling in Bangkok. How often, my darling Ashy, have you had some rose-coloured dreams of settling in South Africa, Australia, Canada or India? How often have you decided to settle somewhere around Manchester? What do you really want? If you ask me to choose between living in Irlam and living in Bangkok, I would choose, without hesitation, to live in Bangkok.'

By the end of September, Tom is at last able to write,

'I hope to start on the first step of my journey home in a few days! – Almost certainly on the boat in about a month from now. You have no idea how excited I am darling.

'It looks as though our unit should enjoy an easy time for a while. The boys certainly deserve it after the hard work of the last three years. I shall certainly be sorry to leave them all but I am just living for the day when I shall set sail for home.

'I wonder if you realise just how much your husband is worrying and thinking about the safest plan for giving you and Jan happiness and security. A job awaits a good English doctor out here. As far as England is concerned I feel that I am one of the many forgotten doctors. I had no time to make a name for myself before I joined the Army so no-one is asking me to come home and join them in any project, but certain people out here are most anxious that I should come out and come quickly. I have been told – 'you will make a fortune if you get in first'.'

Tom receives a parcel from Vera just before he leaves Bangkok. Whether she wrote again after the end of September is not known and if she did the letters have not come to light. Tom writes to thank her for the 'photograph of Jan and the 500 Players No.3.'

'I love the serious photos of Jan especially the very pensive one where she is sitting with her chin resting on her hands.'

On the 9th Tom leaves his unit,

'At very short notice and within a fortnight I should be on the high seas en route for home. They gave me a grand send-off.'

Between the 10th and the 23rd October he sits with others waiting idly in Rangoon, although he did not dare to take time to go to Calcutta to collect his trunk and a diamond 'engagement' ring that he had left there for safety.

'I should reach England about the middle of November. I'll phone you as soon as I possibly can. Meet me – probably in Liverpool or London. – We have waited so patiently for each other throughout these long and wearying months but now it is hard to be patient. Each day seems longer than the last and each rumour re date of departure is met with scornful comment; still no definite news that our ship is coming in at last.'

He is glad that they,

'Saw the job through in Bangkok – we cleared all British POWs before I left.' Tom is also able to spend time with his brother Harold who is stationed nearby – 'he is looking very fit and is looking forward to early demob before Christmas.'

'We may all be home for a real family party at the beginning of the New Year, but I am not really interested in all this. All I want is to get home to you darling as quickly as I can. You must pack your bag ready for an immediate move to wherever we dock. Draw £20 from the bank and keep it handy and when I phone you must fly like the wind to meet me.'

On 21st October he writes,

'I have felt unusually tired and lethargic; it seems that reaction has set in with the relinquishment of all responsibility – I spend most of my time lying on my bed in the camp – too lazy even to think. I try to read and to write letters but I can't concentrate. – I am feeling quite fit and getting very sunburnt. It will be strange for you to see a sunburned husband in the fog of Liverpool or London.

'By the way Ashy, I haven't got any pyjamas at all, let alone warm ones, so see what you can borrow from Eric or Dad for me.

'We are actually going on board today and should sail in a day or two. We should reach England in less than four weeks.'

On the 28th October he writes the last Burma letter. Headed 'at sea'; it is posted in Ceylon.

'We have just called here for a few hours but will have no time to go ashore. This may be my last letter to you from overseas and the next time you hear from me should be over the telephone.'

G.P.Janardanan Nair.
C/Hav. 6732. I.A.M.C.
Meenathethil House.,
Cherukole., MAVELIKARA.P.O.
TRAVANCORE.
(South India.)

Respected Sir,

    After a long time I arrived in 14 C.C.S.,on the 30th December 1945. But I cannot did not saw you. I thought that I can see you in my unit. Any how we people cannot forget you at any time. You made a nice rememberence in the heart of 14 Ind.C.C.S. staff. Now the unit has been disbanded. All personnel posted to other Units. Only few fellows left and awaiting transports to India.

    If you are present with the unit at the last time, that was a biggest help. But GOD didn't allowed it.

    I hope that you are quite O.K. with your family in this time. We also quite happy, and expecting will be release in near future.

    I am very anxious about you, and hope that you never forget we pepole. It sure that we would not meet a Commanding Officer like you again.

    We are leaving Bangkok within a week. That is why I noted my home address in the top of this letter.

    Nothing more to add. I am quite O.K., and wish to the same to you and your family.

    With best wishes.

                          Yours Obediently,

BANGKOK.
5th April.1946.

Letter from a member of C.C.S. staff

140

CHAPTER EIGHT

1945 – 1955

There were no more letters from Vera but, almost fifty years later in response to Karen's question, she wrote down her memories. These are the arrangements that actually were made for Tom's homecoming.

'In October 1945 Ashy was coming home; exactly when he would arrive was very vague so I booked a room at the Park Lane Hotel and I waited till he got there quite late in the evening. We were together again.

'We spent two lovely days in London and then we went to Buxton to see everyone there. Janet had been six months old when her Daddy went away – she was now four and a half and thought that Ashy was her Uncle Eric! She gradually got used to the idea that this was really her Daddy.'

I remember hearing the back door opening into the kitchen at 22 Overdale Avenue. I was playing with Grandma and Grandpa Ashton and Auntie Joyce in the living room. There would have been a coal fire; it was warm and cosy and very safe. The back door opened and I heard a voice – a particular Ashley male voice which I was sure belonged to my Uncle. I knew my Mummy had gone to meet Daddy; I had looked at his photograph every day, written to him, listened to Mummy reading his letters and I had talked about him coming home soon. I felt very shy and I cannot remember anything about him immediately kissing me or picking me up. I have an image in my mind of standing beside him and putting out my hand and seeing it on the trouser leg covering his knee. The day was confused with a great deal of noise and talk and opening of presents. I know I felt quite at ease and included in the happiness of the occasion. I suppose because I still had my grandparents to give me attention I have no memory of feeling left out or missing my mother's company.

'Later, we went up the Moss to see Grandma and Granddad and the rest of the Ashley family.'

The Burma letters reveal the extent of Tom and Vera's anxiety about where they would live, how they would build their family and what they would do after the war. In common with so many other people, they found English life irrevocably changed. The country was in a poor state, rationing of essential everyday items was still in force, the infrastructure of the country was damaged and housing stocks very low. After-shocks from the war years reverberated strongly through the rest of Tom and Vera's lives, and particularly during the six years following their reunion. A certain amount of practical assistance was given to service-people returning from the war, but everyone was expected simply to cope with the 'strange and sudden resumption of normal family life.'

'It is almost as if demobilisation has slipped between two tectonic plates. The historians of the war stop just before it because it is a peace-time event; the historians of the peace pass over it as the final chapter of war-time. – Swords were expected to turn into ploughshares, soldiers into civilians, just like that. The politicians and planners had bigger games to play; the people could sort themselves out. – Men coming back were specifically advised not to talk about their experiences because that was a barrier to reintegrating into family life. Not talk about events that were the most vivid, the most shattering, the most memorable of their lives? – Daddy may have come home but there was a part of him that would never return.'

[Turner and Rennell.Hutchinson.1995.P223]

A Labour Government was elected in July 1945, startling many traditional conservatives. The Welfare State came into being and many doctors opposed the proposal that their terms and conditions should become part of the National Health Service. Rationing became more stringent during 1946 and eventually even bread was rationed. There was so much unrest over the lack of suitable housing that people organised themselves, entering blocks of flats in London and abandoned army camps in the countryside as squatters. The cold weather was extreme during the early months of 1947 and people suffered through a lack of food and heating. The late forties and the fifties were times of austerity and 'making do'. It was not until the Festival of Britain in 1951 and the Coronation of Elizabeth in 1953 that people began to feel really hopeful about the future.

Many of those returning to civilian life became rapidly disillusioned. They missed the excitement and challenge of the war years and they expected more from life, especially as they had missed out on so much already. For some, the only answer seemed to be to seek work abroad.

Throughout his later letters from Burma Tom had expressed his desire to complete his Fellowship of the Royal College of Surgeons, to travel, and to experience life in other countries with his family. Vera remembers,

'After all the reunions we had to consider what we should do. The Medics of Ashy's era were all coming back to civilian life and all looking for jobs. Tom decided to go back to the University to study for his F.R.C.S. It consists of two parts and the Primary has to be passed first. We bought a house in Swinton.'

I started school in the summer of 1942, just after I was five. On the 10th September, Helen, their second 'honeymoon baby', was born. I remember the intense jealousy I felt when she was born, even to the extent that when I was given a present of a book, 'The Water Babies', I thought,

'They've given me this to try to make me feel better, but I don't.'

I think that I was very miserable and sulky for some time. I was a little mollified when I was allowed to give Helen her second name, Christine, the name of a girl I admired at school. I liked school after the first day when my Dad drove to the gates, got out of the car with me,

Tom with Janet, Helen and Roger

showed me into the playground and then, for some inexplicable reason, left me there. Crying, I stood just inside the gate until someone took me into the headmistress's office. Asking me if I could read, she did not believe me when I said I could until she gave me a 'Beacon' book and from it I read the story of the Little Red Hen. I remember thinking what a lot of nonsense it was to read about the 'sky falling down'. I had received much concentrated attention and had been well-taught in Buxton.

I remember quite a lot about living in Swinton; the garden in which I continually jumped and climbed, falling and scraping my elbow badly and feeling very proud that my Dad bandaged it, collecting 'medical things' in a drawer, going upstairs to get a book and knocking over an electric fire in the darkness of a bedroom and screaming in terror because I was sure the carpet would catch fire, Dad bringing home a lemur from the medical School and letting it climb on the mangle. I remember being afraid to go upstairs in the dark but not being able to reach the light switches and dressing by the kitchen fire in the mornings because the bedrooms were so extremely cold.

Tom and Vera's third child, Roger Geoffrey John, was born in Swinton on the 4th March 1948.

Tom was restless and dissatisfied with being back in Manchester and, although by now he had abandoned the idea of making a life in Bangkok, he was strongly drawn to the notion of travelling and working abroad. He recognised that both his own and Vera's parents were aging and that, if they wanted to go abroad, they should do it now. Vera wrote,

'He found it very difficult to settle down. Rationing was still going on, life was busy and we had a car which was good. In 1948 an appointment came up at Makerere College in Uganda. Tom applied and was successful. So, we sold our house and our 'goods and chattels'

and departed hence to Kampala with Janet aged seven, Helen aged two and Roger aged six months. Ashy was going to teach Anatomy and to organise the Medical School which was new.

While we were there, Grandpa Ashton died suddenly of a heart attack one evening while coming back from feeding the hens on his allotment. He was found, lying on the path, by his good friend Ted Gill the butcher.

Janet and Vera, 1948

Helen, Janet, Jonnie and Roger, 1954

Vera described how she felt,

'Very sad – there was no possibility of going home to help or to go to the funeral. Soon after he died, we were coming back to the bungalow one evening in the car. I had my window open and was looking up at the moon and stars. I was aware of a presence passing the open window – I knew that it was my father and that he was saying good-bye. That has stayed with me ever since although I never told anyone about it – not even Ashy. It was an experience which made me feel happy and I was able to accept my father's death and the fact that I would not see him again.

The secondment to Africa was brief.

'The Makerere appointment was for two years so in 1950 we were due home – sans house, sans everything. It was decided that I should go home with the children so that Ashy could pack up the house. We left Lake Victoria in a flying boat in April. I don't recommend travelling on a flying boat with three children; one of them aged two and in nappies. It took us three days to get to Southampton Water, stopping off at Khartoum to refuel at dead of night, on to Sicily and then to Marseilles where we stayed the night because it was rough in the Channel.

'From Southampton we went by bus to London, spending a night there, and then by train to Buxton; back to an English spring. I shall always remember the daffodils and the clean fresh air after the heat of Africa.

'After a few weeks Ashy was home with us. I remember meeting him at Buxton Station – my Darling – I seemed to spend my life meeting him. I was wearing a new dress; it was pink with blue and cream stripes.

Again they had to decide what to do.

'Ashy would return to the University and work for his Primary. We found a house at 12 Circular Road, West Didsbury – an old house with attics and cellars, a coach house and stables. There was a large garden and the house soon became a lovely home. Six months later I was pregnant; Jonathan George was born on the 4th June 1952. We had our home and our family and we were happy. Almost every weekend we saw the family in Buxton or up the Moss and the cousins saw a lot of each other. We had some wonderful holidays in Nevin and Morfa Nevin travelling in our wonderful old Armstrong Siddely.

'Ashy continued to work for his primary and was successful, but it was going to take years to complete his FRCS; it was not easy working for an exam with a young family and while also lecturing at the University. He came back from Africa with a renewed interest in Anatomy, Histology and Embryology so, having been offered a Lectureship in the Medical School, decided to make this his way of life.'

Together again with family, home and career in place, all the things they had agonised over for almost four years, the next chapter of their lives began, and the story of the Burma letters ends.

Postscript

Tom and Vera left a wonderful legacy in their letters, without which this story would not have been told.

I have spent some extra years with my parents, years about which I knew little before I began to edit the letters. Each day I came to my desk with a keen sense of anticipation. Mostly I was delighted, informed and entertained by the words they wrote; at other times I cried and turned away from the poignancy, regret and pain that they expressed, but I was never reluctant to return to follow the story. I didn't want to reach the last letter. With a few books, a very few during a lifetime of reading, it is with extreme reluctance that you turn the final page. I didn't want to read the last of Tom's and Vera's letters. I didn't want the process to be over. Of course, the story is not over, nor did it begin when the letters began. Other family letters, photographs and reminiscences exist which take the story backwards and forwards in time from those war years. Many aspects of this story remain unexplored.

Travelling the Wild Coast of South Africa, Dennis and I visited an artist called Moses. He showed us his work, birds and animals that seemed almost about to move, carved from logs, tree stumps and driftwood. He told us that when he finds a piece of wood he looks at it for some time and eventually the presence of the creature in the wood will become evident to him. He carves as little as possible away until the creature is revealed.

From five hundred letters, I had to carve a lot away in my attempt to produce my interpretation of the essence of the relationship between Tom and Vera and of the circumstances they endured during the war. The letters tell a story against an intense background, within a short time scale, and other family members, experiencing the same events, will have perceived a different picture.

The family tree shows some of the births, marriages and deaths within the families during and after the war years. Some of the deaths have been tragic and premature; by the age of 95, Ada had had to bear the deaths of all three of her sons, none of whom lived to be sixty. Tragedies and joys have affected all sections of the family but it is not possible for them all to be recorded here.

The family spreads its branches wide and the tree spreads wider and wider. Tom and Vera have six grandchildren and eight great-grandchildren. Ada and Fred have twenty one great-grandchildren and thirteen great-great-grandchildren. Emma and Roger have eight great-grandchildren and eight great-great-grandchildren.

The epitaph commemorating the terrible Battle of Kohima has an inscription,

> 'When you go home, tell them of us and say
> For your tomorrow, we gave our today.'

Tom and Vera did not give their lives but, together with many others who experienced such separation, they gave three and a half years of their 'todays'.

Tom and Vera, 1955

Bibliography

Baddiel, D. [2005] *The Secret Purposes* [Abacus]

Binns, Carter and Wood [2000] *Britain at War* [Carlton Books Ltd.]

Bragg, M. [1999] *The Soldier's Return* [Sceptre]

Bryant, A. [1959] *Triumph in the West* [Collins]

Churchill, W. [August 20th1940] *A Speech by the Prime Minister in the House of Commons*

Dunmore, H. [2002] *The Siege* [Penguin]

Garfield, S. [2005] *Our Hidden Lives – The remarkable Diaries of Post-War Britain* [Ebury Press]

Graham, G. and Cole, F. [2001]
Burma Campaign Memorial Library Catalogue & Bibliography [SOAS]

Ismay, Lord. [1969] *The Memoirs of Lord Ismay* [Heinemann]

Journal of the Burma Star Association *DEKHO! - Issues 147 and 148* [2004]

Macdonald Fraser, G. [2001] *Quartered Safe Here* [The Akadine Press]

McEwan, I. [2002] *Atonement* [Vintage]

Mitchell, Prof. G. [1972] *Obituary of G. T. Ashley* [The Manchester Medical Gazette. Vol.51. No.4.]

Owen, F. Lieut. Col. [1946] *The Campaign in Burma* [HMSO]

Ray, J. [2003] *The Illustrated History of World War 2* [Weidenfeld and Nicholson]

Slim, W. Field-Marshall Sir [1956] *Defeat into Victory* [Cassell and Co. Ltd.]

Swinson, A. [1973] *Mountbatten* [Pan/Ballantine]

Thompson, Julian [2002] *The Imperial War Museum Book of the War in Burma* [Pan]

Titford, J. [2003] *Writing Up Your Family History* [Countryside Books]

Turner, B. and Rennell, T. [1995] *When Daddy Came Home* [Hutchinson]

Williams, J. [1950] *Elephant Bill* [Rupert Hart-Davis]